Abide in My Love
Manete in Dilectione Mea
John 15:9

Ascetic and pastoral reflections
for young priests, that they may become
apostles of the Sacred Heart of Jesus

Translated from German by Michael J. Miller

Based on the 6th French edition (Paris: Téqui)

This book was composed shortly after World War I
by an Italian priest who wished to remain anonymous.

Loreto Publications A. D. 2016
Fitzwilliam, NH 03447

Nihil obstat: J. Favre, C.Ss.R., Provincial Superior
Lyons, July 26, 1931

Imprimatur: Maximilian Huard, Vicar General
Verdun, August 2, 1931

2016 English Edition Copyright by
Loreto Publications
P. O. Box 603
Fitzwilliam, NH 03447
www.loretopubs.org
603-239-6671

ISBN: 978-162292-101-0
Printed In USA

*Dedicated to
the "Little Flower" of Lisieux,
so that wherever the fragrance of her "roses" spreads,
this little book might follow too.*

Contents

His Holiness Pius XI to the Author

Our Holy Father, Pope Pius XI, through notes written by His Eminence Cardinal Pacelli, Secretary of State, deigned three times to congratulate, encourage and bless the author of *Manete in dilectione mea:*

"His Holiness hopes that this pious book will be a spiritual aid for souls" (April 8, 1930).

"Tell the author, who wishes to remain unknown, that the service rendered by his works is not unknown to the Holy Father, who hopes that these works will produce all the good that the author himself has in view.... The Apostolic Blessing that the Holy Father sends to this religious priest is intended as a pledge of heavenly favor and a testimony of special benevolence" (Letter to His Excellency Bishop Bartolomasi, Military Ordinary, November 12, 1932).

"May the Lord grant that you may be able to continue devoting your talent and zeal to such a noble purpose and that the help provided to souls through your penetrating, ardent meditations may be the reward for your fruitful activity" (July 15, 1937).

Note to the Reader From the French Translator

These pages, which were first written in Italian, pour out from the heart of a contemplative religious priest who wishes to remain unknown.

They were written down a few years ago.

They were eagerly taken up by the diocesan and religious clergy; they were very cordially praised and recommended by numerous bishops, archbishops and cardinals, encouraged and blessed by the Supreme Shepherd himself; they have spread like a wildfire throughout the world and have already been translated into twenty languages.

One perceives here the beating Heart of Jesus, example, teacher and support of priests.

"Meditate on this golden book," one bishop writes, "and the beating of the Divine Heart will become your own. That is the power of and the reason for its marvelous success."

Since the War, people often speak about *re-enkindling the flame*. May this little book revive in the hearts of priests *the flame* that Jesus has placed within them, with which he wants to enkindle the world through us: "I want my priests to be sowers of love!"[1]

R. H., C.Ss.R.

---

[1] *Au service de Jésus-Prêtre: notes intimes tirées des écrits de mère Louise Marguerite Claret de la Touche* [In the service of Jesus the High Priest: personal notes taken from the writings of Mother Louise Marguerite Claret] (Turin/Rome: Marietti, 1925), published by the *Alliance Sacerdotale universelle des Amis du Sacré-Coeur* [Worldwide Priestly Association of Friends of the Sacred Heart], 2:51.

Note: In the pages of this book, the words of Saint Margaret Mary are quoted from the fourth edition of her complete works: *Vie et oeuvres de sainte Marguerite-Marie Alacoque* [Life and works of St. Margaret Mary Alacoque], 3 vols. (Paris: Librairie J. de Gigord, 1920). This fourth edition reproduces the third edition, published in 1915 by Abp. Gauthey of Besançon, with a few modifications and additions.

Roman numerals indicate the volume, and Arabic numerals the page numbers.

Unless otherwise noted, all footnotes are by the author.

A Little Philosophy of History
Author's Preface To The Seventh Italian Edition

The prophet Samuel arrived in Bethlehem to anoint the new King of Israel in the name of the Lord of Hosts; on that occasion he examined one after the other the sons of Isai (Jesse) but did not find the Lord's Chosen among them. The prophet did not become perplexed, however, since he was certain of the divine promise, but asked Isai whether he had other sons. The father, who had not even taken the trouble to present his youngest son, because he was too small and useless, replied: *"Adhuc reliquus est parvulus et pascit oves,"* "There remaineth yet a young one, who keepeth the sheep." "Send, and fetch him, for we will not sit down till he come hither" (1 Kings 16:11).

Little David came, fearful and out of breath, bewildered on account of this unusual call.... What did the prophet want of him? After all, everyone thought he was scarcely capable of leading the herd of sheep adequately. But Samuel was enlightened by the Holy Ghost, who searches *renes et corda*,[2] looked into the clear, calm eyes of the young shepherd and rejoiced: "Here is the man after God's heart, here is the Lord's anointed!" The voice of him who cannot be deceived whispered into his ear: *"Surge, unge eum, ipse est enim."*[3]

This story is old yet ever new. Anyone who out of ambition or thoughtlessness takes the first place at the Lord's table, runs the risk—today as yesterday, as always—of being humiliated. In contrast, anyone who remains standing at the back of the Temple, like the tax collector, convinced of his own nothingness, ashamed of his own sins, and regarded by himself as unworthy to lift his eyes to heaven, goes home justified.

---

[2] The reins and hearts (Apoc. 2:23).
[3] "Arise, and anoint him, for this is he" (1 Kings 16:12).

Hi in curribus et hi in equis, sang the Psalmist to his golden harp in a triumphant tune, *nos autem in nomine Domini Dei nostri invocabimus.*[4] He who goes into battle with confidence in the One *qui facit mirabilia magna solus*[5], is not far from victory.

This is the spectacle of all ages: the silver trumpets cause the walls of Jericho to collapse; Deborah, without weapons, triumphs over the Canaanites; David strikes down Goliath; Judith revenges with the blood of the loathsome tyrant the tears of her entire people; and young Daniel arises to defend persecuted, slandered innocence against the elders of Juda.... The complete and enormous disproportion between these causes and effects is obvious to the observer at first glance and forces him to wonder in surprise: *Quomodo possunt haec fieri?*[6]

Basically this is a naive question, which deserves no answer but this: "Do you not see that God disregards human events, *ludens in orbe terrarum?*"[7]

Even today the triumphs of truth and justice are reserved primarily to Moses' staff, to Gideon's fleece, to the jawbone of the ass that Manue's son wielded, to David's sling, to Elias' mantle, to Eliseus' staff, to St. Peter's shadow; even today the stone that comes loose from the mountain as though by chance destroys the statue of ungodliness and reduces it to dust.

And why does God work in this way? What can human ignorance answer in the presence of the counsels of the Eternal One? He does what he wills, when he will and in the way he wills—*Dominus est!*[8]

❤

It has been scarcely ten years since this little book was composed. Inspired by obedience, written with faith and love, humble in its outward appearance, devoid of any charism of scholarship or artistry,

---

[4] "Some trust in chariots, and some in horses: but we will call upon the name of the Lord our God" (Ps. 19:8).

[5] "who alone doth great wonders" (Ps. 135:4).

[6] "How can these things be done?" (Jn. 3:9).

[7] "playing in the world" (Prov. 8:31).

[8] "It is the Lord!" (1 Kings 3:18).

it plainly fulfills all the necessary requirements to serve the Lord's glory effectively. In the sense that *quae stulta sunt mundi elegit Deus, ut confundat sapientes; et infirma... et ignobilia... et contemptabilia... et ea quae non sunt, ut ea quae sunt destrueret.*[9]

Nevertheless, the beginnings of this book were not very flattering; God had his plans, and it was to be a *lapis quem reprobaverunt aedificantes.*[10] Yet through Divine Providence it was set on the thorny path of publication and, thanks to the prayers of saintly souls, won the favor of him *qui humilia respicit.*[11] Through this truly undeserved and unexpected fate, the book became a source of overflowing blessings.

Jesus autem intuitus eum, dilexit eum,[12] and since he loved this book, he blessed it and protected it with maternal care and caused it to fly on the wings of love—if I may say so—*usque ad ultimum terrae.*[13]

❤

One day a voice proceeding from a tabernacle entrusted to a poor, simple, unknown soul a magnificent mission: "I want you to serve Me as an instrument to draw souls to My love."[14] And since she replied to him in her naive guilelessness, "I cannot understand how such a thing could happen," the Heart of Jesus said to her: "Through My almighty power, which made everything out of nothing."[15] This makes it clear that God is always the one Author; the creature is only a more or less incapable instrument. Therefore the Lord is jealous of His glory and reserves it entirely for Himself, even though He communicates His gifts to others

---

[9] "But the foolish things of the world hath God chosen, that he may confound the wise; and the weak things... and the base things... and the things that are contemptible... and things that are not, that he might bring to nought things that are" (1Cor. 1:27-28).

[10] "The stone which the builders rejected" (Ps. 117:22).

[11] "looketh down on the low things" (Ps. 112:6).

[12] "And Jesus, looking on him, loved him" (Mk. 10:21).

[13] "even to the uttermost part of the earth" (Acts 1:8).

[14] St. Margaret Mary, II, 193.

[15] St. Margaret Mary, II, 193.

with extravagant generosity. "I chose you," He said to the disciple of His Heart, "as an *abyss of unworthiness and ignorance* for the accomplishment of this great plan, so that everything might come about through Me."[16]

♥

No one would have dared to hope, indeed, would even have thought, that these few simple, unadorned lines would awaken such enthusiasm. As far as I am concerned, I thought that I was already showing them too much honor by passing them on to a few close friends, selected from among the most well-meaning and forbearing, for their pious meditation. St. Teresa of Avila said: "Sometimes I reflect on how our Lord, when He wants something to come about that we do not want, orders things in such a way that we unwittingly become the instrument."[17] Besides, it has been written that Jesus "does not need human efforts, because devotion to His Heart and its reign is spread only through *poor, despised subordinates*, in the midst of contradictions."[18]

This is, in fact, how and why this book, which at most could have counted on becoming a diocesan project, in a short time became as *all-embracing* as Holy Church herself.

I am not taking a bow! After just under three years a second edition appeared, after the book had an incredibly favorable reception from the priests of Italy; after it had been praised by the most competent voices of numerous cardinals and archbishops, after it had been distributed and recommended by countless bishops to their clergy and likewise by a great number of religious superiors to members of their communities, this is now the seventh time that this little book is appearing in its original language.

Meanwhile it has followed the mysterious paths of Divine Providence and crossed the Alps several times, and while France,

---

[16] St. Margaret Mary, II, 70.

[17] Wilhelm Gustav Werner Volk, ed., *Das Buch von den Stiftungen der Kloster der unbeschuhten Carmeliten-Nonnen und die Seelenburg in sieben Wohnungen von der heiligen Theresia von Jesu* (Regensburg: Georg J. Manz, 18692), III, chap. 22, p. 128.

[18] St. Margaret Mary, II, 478.

Germany, Poland, Spain, Hungary, Czechoslovakia, England, Holland, Portugal, Lithuania, and Japan one after the other translated it into their respective languages, Yugoslavia prepared two editions, one in Croatian and the other in Slovenian. Austria, Switzerland and Belgium likewise gave it a good reception. In Ireland, Albania, Bulgaria and recently in Denmark, Finland, Norway and Sweden, it found friends, protectors, and apostles.

It has crossed the oceans, as though it had been driven to do so by an invisible hand; it has met with sympathy and quick acceptance in Libya, Somalia, Eritrea, Palestine, Egypt, Algeria, Sudan, Abyssinia, Uganda, the Congo, on the Ivory Coast, on the island of Madagascar and in the English colonies on the Cape.

Not even the stormy ocean stopped it, and while it was drawing near to Canada and the U.S.A., it shyly, silently entered the territories of Argentina, Chile, Paraguay, Columbia, Uruguay, Bolivia, Peru, Ecuador, and Venezuela and spread there among the clergy. It brought new supplies of confidence and zeal for Catholic priests even into far-off Alaska and forgotten Tierra del Fuego.

It mocked the high-handed oversight of an Anti-Christ of sorrowful memory and crossed the borders of Mexico; thus it brought hope and consolation to those who profess the faith... and after it had made its way by a thousand different paths into China, India, and Korea, it approached the distant coasts of Australia and, as *herald of the great king*, reached the Philippines, Siam, Burma, New Guinea, and even the Malaysian Peninsula and the countless little islands of Oceania: *Eris testis illius ad omnes homines!*[19]

When I, quite abashed, see the miraculous multiplication of this modest bread for priestly souls and am compelled to repeat to these friends throughout the world: *Gratias ago Deo meo, quod omnium vestrum lingua loquor,*[20] what better could I do than to keep myself hidden, so as not to hinder the mysterious plans of Providence. "Learn," said Jesus to the favored messenger of His Divine Heart, "that the more you withdraw into your nothingness, the more My greatness condescends to find you."[21]

---

[19] "Thou shalt be his witness to all men" (Acts 22:15).

[20] "I thank my God I speak with all your tongues" (1Cor. 14:18, Vulgate). Modern translations of the Scripture verse read: "I thank God that I speak in tongues more than you all."

[21] St. Margaret Mary, II, 139.

With the humility that prepares the ways of the Lord I would like to increase this trust, which allows room for neither discussions nor debates and grows in proportion to the difficulties that it encounters: Is this not just a fruit, the first fruit of love? *Caritas omnia credit, omnia sperat, omnia sustinet.*[22] Therefore in the little adversities, in the many obstacles that are never lacking in the works of God, I consider trust as the best weapon. These too are the Redeemer's words: "Fear nothing, trust in Me. I am your protector. Then you will not lack help until My Heart lacks power."[23]

❤

It was necessary to give this new edition, which probably is not the last, a more careful and, if possible, definitive form. In my opinion the book was significantly improved. So I hope that the piety of my good readers will find great profit in it.

O young servants of God, receive these thoughts, which my fraternal devotion to you has compiled; ... on these pages my whole soul can be found: *argentum et aurum non est mihi, quod autem habei, hoc tibi do.*[24]

May Mary Immaculate, the priestly Virgin, form your heart after the model of the adorable Heart of the eternal High Priest and grant that you may derive from reading it abundant fruits of sanctification for yourself and for the salvation of souls.

A useless servant of the Most Sacred Heart of Jesus

---

[22] "Charity... believeth all things, hopeth all things, endureth all things" (1Cor. 13:7).

[23] St. Margaret Mary, II, 194.

[24] "Silver and gold I have none; but what I have, I give thee" (Acts 3:6).

Recommendations

Recommendation by His Eminence Cardinal Piffl, Archbishop of Vienna

He who is called by Providence to the priestly state must honestly strive to conform his heart more and more each day to the Heart of Jesus.

Devotion to the Most Sacred Heart of Jesus is the best way to do this. It will help him to preserve the grace of fidelity to his vocation and of conscientious fulfillment of his duties and fill him with that cooperative apostolic attitude which, for the love of Jesus, looks after the poor, the sick, and the sinful whenever possible.

Therefore the present booklet, *Manete in dilectione mea,* which simply and cordially seeks to win priests over to devotion to the Most Sacred Heart of Jesus, should be given to every newly ordained priest as a guide and companion in his priestly life.

Vienna, March 3, 1926

+ Friedrich Gustav Cardinal Piffl
Archbishop of Vienna

Recommendation of His Excellency Archbishop Ignatius Rieder

The little book with the beautiful title *Manete in dilectione mea* is a wake-up call to priests, especially to young priests, through which they are invited with kindly words to come to the Heart of the Savior, so as to learn from this Heart love, zeal for souls, and all the sentiments that should adorn a priest.

This dear little book, which has already been widely circulated in Italy and France, is hereby recommended all the more because in our times, in which so much external activity is demanded of priests, they need interior recollection and quiet rest upon the Heart of Jesus. May my blessing accompany it!

Salzburg, March 18, 1926
Ignatius Rieder,
Archbishop

Recommendation of His Grace Viktor Bieler, Bishop of Sitten

The little book *Manete in dilectione mea* is an urgent call to all priests to become acquainted with devotion to the Most Sacred Heart of Jesus, to practice it, and to spread it among the faithful. In noble language it presents the most important motives capable of convincing and inspiring priests to take up this devotion to the Most Sacred Heart of the Redeemer. No one will be able to resist the persuasive and stirring words of the author; therefore we consider this little book practical and commendable.

Sitten, Good Friday 1926
+ Viktor
Bishop of Sitten

Preface

To the third edition by His Excellency Archbishop Alexius M. Lepicier, former General Superior of the Servants of Mary, Titular Archbishop of Tarsus, Apostolic Visitator of the East Indies

Divine Providence, which watches over the destiny of the elect and guides and leads everything for their good according to number, measure and weight, in recent decades has caused devotion to the Most Sacred Heart of Jesus, our adorable God and sweet Savior, to increase and grow in quite an extraordinary way among the Christian people. This beautiful devotion reminds us of the immeasurable love of the divine Redeemer and of the bitter pains that He suffered for us; consequently it is a powerful incentive for us, who have been redeemed with His precious Blood, to love such an amiable Lord in return with our whole heart and our whole soul and to serve Him with our whole strength. At the same time, by keeping this adorable Heart before our eyes with its magnificent examples of goodwill, self-denial and patience, this salutary devotion encourages us to be more generous in the service of God, humbler in our self-appraisal, more mortified in our way of life, more lenient with the mistakes of our fellow men, more patient in adversities, more inclined to forgive when we have suffered injustice, and always ready to return good for evil.

If this devotion is already so abundantly useful for the Christian people, then for the priest, who in his life and love and activity among the faithful must be another Christ—*sacerdos alter Christus*—it is of downright capital importance to study, worship and love the Most Sacred Heart of Jesus, to clothe himself in Its virtues and to strive to imitate the divine life that has so greatly glorified the Father, gladdened the angels and bestowed on the Church such a wealth of gifts.

The author of this little book *Manete in dilectione mea,* who is full of holy, wise zeal, has therefore accomplished an extremely holy work by challenging the priests of the New Covenant to become more closely attached to the adorable Heart of Jesus, to be nourished by His life and to arrange their entire being according to His thoughts and wishes.

We therefore recommend most cordially this little book to priests, especially the newly ordained, whose hearts are filled with a great and noble love for Him who was "wounded for our iniquities, bruised for our sins."

Rev. Alexius M. Lepicier, O.S.M.
Archbishop of Tarsus

Abide in My Love
Manete in Dilectione Mea

… et nos credidimus charitati …
… and we … have believed the charity which God hath to us
(1 John 4:16)

Tristis Est Anima Mea[25]

Angel of God, what can this moving lament mean, which constantly reaches our ear from all the tabernacles of the world: *Tristis est anima mea usque ad mortem?*[26]

---

[25] "My soul is sorrowful" (Mt. 26:38).

[26] "My soul is sorrowful even unto death" (Mt 26:38). In heaven—and consequently in the tabernacle also—Jesus is glorified and can no longer suffer. But even though He is incapable of suffering, He certainly cannot be indifferent about whether He receives honor or insults from His creatures. When we speak about the sorrows of His Heart, then, as though they were present, we express an idea that certainly does not correspond to reality, yet which is thoroughly in keeping with Catholic Tradition. In fact the Heart of Jesus that suffered during His earthly life is exactly the same Heart that is in heaven and in the Most Blessed Sacrament. We say that It suffers as a way of indicating that He suffered when He was able to suffer. And He not only endured the physical and moral pains involved in His mission as Redeemer, but also agonized because of His clear, exact and discerning foresight of all the sins that would be committed until the end of time. Day after day our wickedness forces Him to witness these offspring of our ingratitude, these triumphal processions of godlessness, which twenty centuries ago caused His Heart to tremble and which are so terrible that they would renew His sorrowful Passion if He were not already glorified.

1

I see neither the horrible instruments of torture that mangled the spotless body of the God-man, nor do I see the large cup overflowing with bitterness....

And the Angel of the Eucharist answers:[27] The reason for this complaint is the unbearable, incomprehensible, utterly unjustified indifference of the Christian people toward the One who is the center of love and the source of life, toward this *Heart which has loved*

This is the sense in which we should understand the words of St. Margaret Mary about the Seraphim who pay honor to the Sacred Heart of Jesus "in order to atone for the profound bitterness that He endured and still endures in the Most Blessed Sacrament, as a result of the ingratitude and indifference of mankind" (St. Margaret Mary, II, 288). See also other occurrences of the expression which put the question in the correct light (*ibid.*, II, 116, 152, 153).

As a final word on this question, we add the following remarks: Even though Jesus *can no longer suffer today* for the failings of mankind, *He still rejoices* to see our acts of reparation and atonement, because His glorified state does not rule out the possibility of ever new increases in accidental happiness. They cause Him joy, because they testify to our love for Him, because they counterbalance the sins of today that He deplores so much, and they strive to console Him for the sufferings of His Passion, which He has not forgotten. Moreover our works of atonement and our reparations have a retroactive effect as well: Jesus saw them during His earthly life, and He was *consoled by them then*; today they still cause Him joy on account of the consolation that they gave Him *then*.

Therefore Our Lord recommended to St. Margaret Mary the practice of making a *Holy Hour* in order to alleviate the bitterness that He experienced in the Garden of Olives (Gauthey, I, 126). On this topic, see Jean Vincent Bainvel, *Devotion to the Sacred Heart: The Doctrine and Its History* (London: Burns Oates and Washbourne, 1926), Part 2, Chapter 1, §9, and Jean-Baptiste Terrien, S.J., *La dévotion au Sacré-Coeur de Jésus, d'après les documents authentiques et la théologie* [Devotion to the Sacred Heart of Jesus according to the original sources and theology] (Paris: Lethielleux).

[27] St. Margaret Mary speaks about angels who are instructed to watch over the Most Blessed Sacrament (II, 109, 167, 539). According to Fr. Faber, the Archangel Michael revealed to St. Eutropius that he had been sent by God to guard the Holy Eucharist (cf. Frederick William Faber, *The Blessed Sacrament: or the Works and Ways of God* (London: Thomas Richardson and Son, 1856), 517 f.

mankind so tenderly... yet in return receives nothing but ingratitude, contempt, sacrileges, irreverence and indifference.[28]

But that is still not all; there is another far more painful reason for Jesus' grief in the Most Blessed Sacrament. For one of the causes, perhaps the most important cause of this regrettable behavior of so many souls toward the Divine Heart is—dare I say it?—the indifference of some of the clergy. Poor Jesus! Souls consecrated to Him treat Him this way![29]

Reflect on these words, O reader; and with regard to this very painful phenomenon, which however is widespread everywhere, might you be obliged to repeat the mighty word of a great bishop: *Causa sunt ruinae populi, sacerdotes mali?*[30]

Painful Facts

It was in June of 1902; a holy soul was spending time before the tabernacle adoring the Sacrament of love; it was a day of graces and blessings....

Jesus' voice could be heard clearly, and it whispered into her ear these words from Paradise: "If priests only knew what treasures of love for them My Heart contains within it!... Margaret Mary proclaimed My Heart to the world; as for you, announce it to My priests; let My priests know about it; draw them all to My Heart.... I need them in order to carry out My work.... My Heart is the chalice of My Blood: If anyone has the duty and the right to drink from this chalice, is it not first of all the priest, who every day at the altar brings the chalice to his lips? ... Therefore he should come to My Heart and drink!"[31]

---

[28] St. Margaret Mary, I, 137; II, 72, 103.

[29] St. Margaret Mary, I, 137; II, 72, 103.

[30] Bad priests are the reason for the corruption of the people (St. Gregory the Great, *Epistola LXIX ad Brunechildem reginam*, PL 77, 1209).

[31] Mother Louise Marguerite Claret de la Touche, see *Au service de Jésus-Prêtre: notes intimes tirées des écrits de mère Louise Marguerite Claret de la Touche* (Turin and Rome: Marietti, 1925); reprinted by the *Alliance Sacerdotale universelle des Amis du Sacré-Coeur* [World Priestly Association of Friends of the Sacred Heart], 2:47-49. The reader can learn about this association, its founding, spirit and organization either at the Basilica of the Sacred Heart on Montmartre, Paris, or at the headquarters of the work, Betania Del Sacro Cuore, in Vische Canavese (Aosta), Italy.

Since then have not *all* priests come accordingly, so as to drink from the Most Sacred Heart of Jesus, as Jesus desires?

Unfortunately no. This is a sad fact, the result of everyday experience. How many priests are there then, who have and practice a true, substantial and steadfast devotion to the Sacred Heart of Jesus; how many spread it zealously and preach it constantly?

Let us search for the completely obvious reason for all this decline, all these scandals, this alarmingly increase of godlessness, for this wave of immorality and filth that sweeps everything along with it, not just outside the Church.... *Ideo inter vos multi infirmi..., et dormiunt multi.*[32]

And yet priestly life is supposed to be thoroughly imbued with the pleasing fragrance of Jesus Christ; it is supposed to be nothing but an intimate, continuous, generous, perfect, uninterrupted exchange of love between the Heart of God and the heart of man: *"Qui diligit me, diligetur a Patre meo, et ego diligam eum, et manifestabo ei meipsum."*[33] Someone once wrote that we priests are "chalices filled with Jesus and designed to pour Jesus into souls". Now who can comprehend how much love this twofold task presupposes: to be filled with the Spirit of Jesus and to give it to the world?

But this intimate, sincere love, which for us is a *duty of our state in life,* as you see, is also a debt of gratitude in the strict sense, an inner need and a right of the heart. But look at all that Jesus has done for His priests! What a wealth of graces He gave them by preserving them in so many dangers for their vocation, what tender intimacy He then showed them in calling them, and then in consecrating them! *De tenebris vos vocabit in admirabile lumen suum.*[34]

The daring metaphor, "to drink from the Heart of Jesus," with which the great mystics of the Middle Ages were so familiar, is found in the Gospel: *Si quis sitit veniat ad me et bibat* (Jn. 7:37): "If any man thirst, let him come to me and drink." St. Peter Canisius said, concerning the vision that he had had on September 4, 1549, in St. Peter's Basilica in Rome: "Lord, while showing me Your Sacred Heart, You commanded me to drink from this spring of salvation" (cf. Otto Braunsberger, *Beati Petri Canisii, Societatis Jesu, Epistolae et acta,* 8 vols. [Freiburg, 1896-1923], 1:54).

[32] "Therefore are there many infirm and weak among you: and many sleep" (1Cor. 11:30).

[33] "He that loveth me shall be loved of my Father: and I will love him and will manifest myself to him" (Jn. 14:21).

[34] "[He] hath called you out of darkness into his marvellous light" (1Pet. 2:9).

Where to begin in describing the trust that He has shown us? He has entrusted everything to us, the most precious things in heaven and on earth: the Church, souls, His Body, His Precious Blood, His adorable Heart, His Immaculate Mother, the golden keys of His paradise, along with full spiritual authority to bind and loose; and in the two most sublime actions of our ministry He deigns to lend us His own person, so to speak: *Ego te absolvo... Hoc est Corpus meum...* [I absolve you... This is My Body....] Sanctifying grace has already made us so great, *divinae consortes naturae!* [35] Yet such a magnificent elevation seems not to be enough for His Heart; He makes us miracle workers and redeemers like Himself: *Ecce dedi te in lucem gentium, ut sis salus mea usque ad extremum terrae.* [36]

And how often has He called us, how many invitations, how many counsels, how many instructions has He bestowed on us! He has instructed us about all and sundry; He wanted to keep no secrets from us: *Omnia quaecumque audivi a Patre meo, nota feci vobis.* [37]

Think of the moving, trusting statements that He made to St. Margaret Mary: "I thirst ardently to be honored by men in the Blessed Sacrament, and I find *almost no one* who tries, according to My desire, to slake My thirst by making Me some return! ... Do thou, at least, give Me the consolation of supplying for their ingratitude as far as thou art able... with the merits of My Sacred Heart." [38] "The Eternal, the Incomprehensible, the Infinite stretches out His hand to me, His almighty hand extended to a creature.... With a sublime gesture He requests from His creature its treasures of devotion and compassion as an alms.... He implores His creature with gentle emphasis and moving tenderness: 'Love is not loved.... *You at least*, love Me!'"

You may say that He was not thinking of the ministers in His sanctuary when He made this complaint. Oh, He certainly was thinking of them, since He says: "See the wounds that I receive from *my chosen people*... The others are content to beat My Body,

---

[35] "Partakers of the divine nature" (2 Pet. 1:4).

[36] "Behold, I have given thee to be the light of the Gentiles, that thou mayst be my salvation even to the farthest part of the earth" (Isa. 49:6).

[37] "All things whatsoever I have heard of my Father, I have made known to you" (Jn. 15:15).

[38] St. Margaret Mary, II, 604 and 580; the concluding phrase "with the merits..." appears on II, 84.

but they, the priests, attack My Heart."[39] And how right He was to accuse us of lukewarmness, since justice demands *more love* from someone *who has received more benefits*.[40]

And although He could demand so much of us, what does He want from us in return for His gifts?

Open the Sacred Scriptures, *scrutamini Scripturas*.[41] There you read the answer: *Praebe, fili mi, cor tuum mihi*.[42] He demands of us—directly at least—neither profound knowledge nor money, nor works of penance, nor night vigils, nor heroic acts of virtue; first and foremost He wants us to love Him: *Dilige, et quod vis fac*.[43]

But unfortunately even today we can repeat the saying of St. Gregory with the same heart-rending truth: *Ecce mundus sacerdotibus plenus est; tamen in messe Dei rarus valde invenitur operator, quia officium quidem sacerdotale sumpsimus, sed opus officii non implemus*.[44] There is a lack of true laborers, because among us one so rarely finds the supernatural, unselfish love that never says, "That is enough"; the love that "makes easy all that is difficult and bears burdens with equanimity".[45]

To each and every minister of His sanctuary the Lord unceasingly poses this unsettling question, which hurls lightning bolts of revelation into the very depths of the soul: *Diligis me plus his?*[46] And only when He hears an affirmative answer as the honest

---

[39] St. Margaret Mary, III, 175. How these wounds correspond to our time can be understood from another very well-known passage; see footnote 26 of this little work.

[40] See Lk. 7:42.

[41] "Search the scriptures" (Jn. 5:39).

[42] "My son, give me thy heart" (Prov. 23:26).

[43] "Love, and do what you want" (St. Augustine, *In epistolam Ioannis ad Parthos; tractatus* VII [1Jn. 4:4-12], cap. 4, n. 8; PL 35, 2033).

[44] "Behold, the world is full of priests; nevertheless one rarely finds a laborer in God's harvest, indeed because we accept the priestly office but do not carry out the work of the office" (St. Gregory the Great, *Homilia XVII in Evangelia: Habita ad episcopos in fontes Lateranensium* [Lk. 10:1-9], I, 3; PL 76, 1139).

[45] Thomas à Kempis, *The Imitation of Christ*, Book III, Chapter 5.

[46] "Lovest thou me more than these?" (Jn. 21:15).

expression of a sweet reality—only then does He declare us worthy of our office: *Pasce agnos meos.*[47]

He demands of us *love*, but understands well that He cannot be content with just any cold, feeble, inconstant, calculating and selfish love: *Oportet amantem omnia dura et amara propter dilectum libenter amplecti.*[48] Instead He wants an ardent, zealous, constant, willing and active love, which is a living image of that mighty and mysterious fire that He brought to earth by taking on a human heart. *Dilige me plus his? ... ex toto corde tuo, ex tota anima tua, ex tota mente tua, ex tota virtute tua?*[49] O priest, He seems to say, every day you lift up the divine sacrificial Lamb in profound silence and in the pleasing fragrance of incense; "for the lips of the priest shall keep knowledge, and they shall seek the law at his mouth: because he is the angel of the Lord of hosts."[50] You forgive and condemn, you admonish and teach *tanquam potestatem habens*,[51] but look at those pious women at the back of the church who offer up their fervent prayers, look at those innocent girls, look at those old sinners who like the laborers at the last hour dedicate themselves today to My service in the love of their renewed Christian life and are as though newly baptized in repentance.... Look at them all and then answer the One who probes the mind and conscience: Do you love me more than these? ... More than every single one of them? ... More than all of them taken together? ... *Diligis me plus his?*

Oh, He is still waiting for the answer.... Poor Jesus! He seems to be sad and troubled: *Plangit enim eos, qui nesciunt cur plangantur.* [52]

---

[47] "Feed my lambs" (Jn. 21:15).

[48] "He that loveth must willingly embrace all that is hard and bitter, for the sake of his Beloved" (Thomas à Kempis, *The Imitation of Christ*, Book III, Chapter 5).

[49] Lovest thou me more than these? ... with thy whole heart and with thy whole soul and with thy whole mind and with thy whole strength?" (Jn. 21:15 and Mk. 12:30).

[50] Mal. 2:7.

[51] "As one having power [authority]" (Mk. 1:22).

[52] "He laments those who do not know why they are being lamented" (St. Gregory the Great, *Homilia XXXIX in Evangelia: Habita ad populum in basilica beati Joannis, quae dicitur Constantiniana* [Lk. 19:42-47], II, 3; PL 76, 1295).

The Forgotten God

Tell me, how is it that so many of us wittingly and deliberately stay away from the tabernacle and, when their ministry compels them to approach it, their hearts are almost always somewhere else? Might it not be because they are secretly storing other treasures elsewhere?

Why do many unwise priests set aside the fruitful, sanctifying recollection of prayer, instead of taking in hand with a joyful heart the sound, powerful, traditional activity of Catholicism, which presupposes so much heroic purification and fosters so much magnanimous progress of the soul? Why do they not applaud this "piety ... which, by prayer, word of mouth, by the religious press, by personal example, by works of charity, seeks in every way possible to lead souls to the Sacred Heart of Jesus and to restore to the same Sacred Heart His sovereign rule over the family and over society"?[53] Instead they fritter away their energies in feverish, foolish work which they tout as *Catholic Action*—isn't that ironic? Do not misunderstand me: Authentic Catholic Action, the kind that is encouraged and blessed by the Supreme Shepherds, the fruit of an ardent interior life, enlivened by prayer, obedience and sacrifice, is one of the most brilliant crowns of Holy Mother the Church. But it has nothing to do with that tasteless sort of activity of questionable origin; the latter in fact is characterized by dubious airs and obviously naturalistic and sometimes even materialistic tendencies while it boldly and recklessly frolics in the vicinity of the yawning pits of Americanism and Modernism.... This is nothing but a dangerous illusion, a pointless noise, a sickly deterioration and a desacralization of the true apostolate. It separates souls forever from Jesus Christ, for plainly it is not concerned about the efficacy of all-powerful grace and it strives to remove the shepherd and his flock from the beneficial influence of the adorable Heart.

Why in fact do so many *task forces, committees, gatherings* and *congresses*, which gobble up so much money and effort, not give Christian life in our time all the support that we might in fairness expect of them? Do you know why? Because many times the *center of gravity* is off! Didn't Paul say about our Lord: *Omnia in ipso constant?*[54] Just as everything in the material world was

---

[53] Pius XI, Encyclical *Ubi arcano Dei* (23 December 1922), n. 54.
[54] "By him all things consist" (Col.1:17).

created through Him, so too in the spiritual world everything has its ultimate foundation and starting point in Him; consequently everything without exception must rely on Him, the general and essential goal of the whole universe: *Filium suum unigenitum misit Deum in mundum, ut vivamus per eum.*[55] Unfortunately this firmly established, dynamic law of souls is so often infringed that the order established by Divine Providence is necessarily overturned and the social equilibrium is seriously endangered.

Catholics work, sometimes *even too much*, but often with a merely human outlook and human methods, without allowing our Lord to exert His beneficial, all-encompassing attraction. This plays out accordingly in the life of souls, and to what a great extent, my God! Here we are talking about a deep-rooted disorder, the results of which are dissolution and destruction. This is a depressing, worrisome phenomenon of suffocation, emptiness and decline: *Scimus autem, quod omnis creatura ingemiscit ... usque adhuc.*[56]

For how many of us, *dicebam vobis, nunc autem et flens dico,*[57] has the extremely meek Heart of the Redeemer largely lost its attraction! We are interested only in our little selves, occupied completely by our miserable plans; every day we seek the idol of our ego, which robs God of the gifts of incense and sacrifice and all too often claims a ridiculous infallibility and sets up a throne for itself. The Apostle could also say about us: *Velamen positum est super cor eorum.*[58]

But the worst is yet to come! And who would believe it, if it were not enough to open your eyes to be convinced of it? Some go so far as to neglect their prayer, meditation, and examination of conscience, on the pretext of working more for souls. With disturbing carelessness they surrender the foundations of the interior life; unscrupulously and unhesitatingly they demolish the traditional bulwark of piety, so as to be able to devote more time to external activity..., and thereby—*veritatem dico in Christo, non mentior*[59]—they still think that they are honoring God more.

---

[55] "God hath sent his only begotten Son into the world, that we may live by him" (1Jn. 4:9).

[56] "For we know that every creature groaneth and travaileth in pain, even till now" (Rom. 8:22).

[57] "I have told you often and now tell you weeping" (Phil. 3:18).

[58] "The veil is upon their heart" (2Cor. 3:15).

[59] "I speak the truth in Christ; I lie not" (Rom. 9:1).

How often while meditating on the serious words that our Holy Father has often repeated in reference to the importance of the interior life, have I thought of you young priests, who through real or even imagined necessity have let yourselves be swept along. Misled by deceptive sophistries, you have spent your best years under the all-too-heavy yoke of countless projects, projects that demand and consume all your physical and moral strength. And while I speak today to you, who are sleep-deprived and breathless in the general confusion and disorder of crazy, unproductive activity, losing your peace and salvation, your taste and sense for the things of God... I ask you with anguish of soul: Why do you want to continue dedicating yourself to such a useless expense of your precious energies, to so many spiritual ruins with such paltry success?

The famous statesman Donoso Cortés quite correctly said—certainly you remember it—that things in the world are constantly getting worse "because there are more battles than prayers"! And yet you consider it a claim to glory that you no longer have a single moment free to attend to the most urgent necessity, to remedy the constant decay of an arid, restless spirit that day by day continues to lose its fine, pleasing fragrance of Christ, *dissipavit substantiam suam.*[60]

Oh, I know, I know very well: You are working wonders in the field of Catholic Action, your name is on everyone's lips; I read in the newspapers the high praises of your work; I see you hurry by, out of breath, your forehead bathed in apostolic sweat... I am almost tempted to wonder what the dear Lord would do—poor fellow!—if He did not have you.

Believe me this time at least, because I know something about the matter: You are running well, but out of the path! *Magnae vires et cursus celerrimus praeter viam.*[61]

There are too many projects, too much business, too many things that are incompatible with your priestly ministry, too much dreaming, too much noise, too much work! There is a lack of order in the dizzying train of your thoughts, a lack of logical

---

[60] "[He] wasted his substance" (Lk. 15:13).

[61] "...great efforts and very swift running but out of the path" (St. Augustine, *Enarrationes in Psalmos XXXI: Enarratio II: Sermo ad plebem,* no. 4; PL 36, 259).

coherence in the sequence of your actions, a lack of practical direction in your life, no compass on your ship; your body lacks a soul: *Ubi es, quando tibi ipsi praesens non es? Et quando omnia percurristi, quid, te neglecto, profecisti?*[62]

Your whole being is oddly split apart, and along with the anarchy of the mind, uneasiness and confusion rule within you. Your power to resist the reprehensible flatteries of the flesh is diminishing; your soul gets in contact with reality less and less often and only superficially....; and this leads to ever more serious compromises and ever more frequent concessions to worldly demands. And finally you arrive at a humiliating capitulation of your priestly dignity to the spirit of the world.... Peace flees from your heart and a solemn moral bankruptcy will necessarily be the consequence of such a state of affairs. *Sollicita es, et turbaris erga plurima!*[63]

Excusationes in Peccatis[64]

What? Do you seriously believe that you will save souls that way?

I know that you live in the shadow of this disastrous illusion and that you—more or less honestly—strive to justify this foolish behavior against the objections of your conscience. *Confidis teipsum esse ducem caecorum, lumen eorum qui in tenebris sunt, eruditorem insipientium, magistrum infantium, habentem formam scientiae et veritatis in lege.*[65] Well, then,

---

[62] "Where art thou when thou art not present to thyself? And when thou hast considered all things, what profit will it be to thee if thou hast neglected thyself?" (Thomas à Kempis, *The Imitation of Christ*, Book II, Chapter 5).

[63] "Thou art careful [full of cares] and art troubled about many things" (Lk. 10:41).

[64] Sinning wantonly. (See Ps. 140/141:4: "Incline not my heart to evil words: to make excuses in sins with men that work iniquity: and I will not communicate with the choicest of them.)

[65] "[Thou] art confident that thou thyself art a guide of the blind, a light of them that are in darkness, an instructor of the foolish, a teacher of infants, having the form of knowledge and of truth in the law" (Rom. 2:19-20).

you should know what the Abbot of Clairvaux thinks of your feverish work, the vertiginous running around, the tense frenzy in which you are leading your miserable life: *Perdis tempus; in his stulto labore consumeris, quae non sunt nisi afflictio spiritus, evisceratio mentis, evacuatio gratiae.*[66]

Just look at how justified this accusation is! Did not the Angelic Doctor of the Church write: *Qui divinis ministeriis applicantur ... perfecti in virtute esse debent?*[67]

We do not wish to pass rash judgment, but one could almost say that you are still far away, even increasingly far away from this perfection of your state in life... *ignorantes Jesum.*[68] And yet you speak about it so eloquently! *Qui ergo alium doces, teipsum non doces?*[69]

One is tempted to think—excuse me for saying so—that you are not convinced by what you teach...; one could say that you are afraid of God; ... one could say that Jesus is not with you, nor you with Him!

And yet the first steps of your priesthood were full of the best hopes: *Quomodo cecidisti de caelo, Lucifer?*[70]

Youth ministry, newspapers, movies, splendid sermons, campaigning for elections, dramatic presentations, sacred music... and also secular academies, scholarly publications, academic degrees and diplomas..., all of these things that are in themselves good and occupations that are often necessary..., but woe to those who surrender themselves completely to them, without keeping back something for themselves; woe to those who on account of

---

[66] "You are wasting your time; you are being consumed by foolish labor in these matters that are nothing but torment of the spirit, the gutting of the mind and the loss of grace" (St. Bernard of Clairvaux, *De consideratione ad Eugenium III. Papam,* I, 2: *Vis consuetudinis ad inducendos praves mores, et duritiam cordis;* PL 182, 731).

[67] "Those who dedicate themselves to divine ministries ... must be perfect in virtue" (St. Thomas Aquinas, *In IV libros Sententiarum Magistri Petri Lombardi expositio, distinctio* XXIV, q. 3, art. 1).

[68] "... not knowing him (Jesus)" (Acts 13:27).

[69] "Thou therefore, that teachest another, teachest not thyself" (Rom. 2:21).

[70] "How art thou fallen from heaven, O Lucifer" (Isa. 14:12).

them lose sight of the *unum necessarium* [the one thing necessary]! "[Jesus] has no need of our works but only of our *love*."[71]

For God's sake, do you ever really think about the fact that, when all is said and done—or better yet, first and foremost—you too have a soul that has to be saved? A soul that hungers for truth, thirsts for justice and is fed by "every word that proceedeth from the mouth of God"?[72] Do you reflect that in the innermost depths of your heart a wonderful guest is staying, who waits there for signs of respect from your heart? Do you know that the dwelling of the Holy Ghost in the soul of a just man is no less real and no less certain than the presence of Jesus in the Eucharist?[73]

Are you convinced that every human being in the state of grace is a precious dwelling place of the living God? That to *grieve* this gentle Consoler, to *resist Him habitually* and finally to *extinguish* Him, as the Apostle puts it,[74] is tantamount to denying in practice Catholic theology and the dogma of redemption?

It is true, you have kept the orthodox faith—at least until now; but do you really think that before the judgment seat from which there is no appeal, it will be enough to justify yourself with the *verbum auditum et non factum, cognitum et non amatum, creditum et non servatum*?[75]

And what does it profit a man "to gain the whole world" for God, if he then went on to lose paradise? *Dico enim vobis, quia nisi*

---

[71] St. Thérèse of the Child Jesus, *Story of a Soul*, Translated by John Clarke, O.C.D., ch. 9, p. 189, 3rd. ed. Washington D.C., ICS Publications, 1996

[72] Mt. 4:4.

[73] In the revelations granted to St. Mechthilde, Jesus compares His presence in the soul that is in the state of grace with His presence under the consecrated species (*Liber specialis gratiae* [The Book of Special Grace], Part 6, chapter 11).

[74] "Extinguish not the spirit" (1 Thess. 5:19); "You always resist the Holy Ghost" (Acts 7:51); "Grieve not the holy Spirit of God" (Eph. 4:30). I wish that every one of my readers could meditate on the volume by Raoul Plus, S.J., *God Within Us*, translated by Edith Cowell (London: Burns Oates & Washbourne, 1945).

[75] "The word which I have heard and not fulfilled, which I have known and not loved, which I have believed and not observed" (cf. Thomas à Kempis, *The Imitation of Christ*, Book III, Chapter 2).

abundaverit justitia vestra plus quam scribarum et pharisaeorum, non intrabitis in regnum caelorum.[76]

Do not object that Jesus Himself spent long years working uninterruptedly in His Father's field, *praedicans et evangelizans.*[77] Have you not read that his "food was to do the will of God"?[78] Don't you remember that during His short earthly life He was so to speak completely immersed in perpetual prayer: *erat pernoctans in oratione Dei?*[79]

Do not object either that St. Paul too, that exalted example of every type of apostolate, was quite crushed beneath the weight of his tremendous, difficult work, *instantia mea quotidiana, sollicitudo omnium ecclesiarum.*[80] Of course he unreservedly spent himself in the service of the truth, *abundantius omnibus laboravi;*[81] but you forget all too easily that Jesus was his habitual thought, his constant occupation, his normal breathing, *mihi vivere Christus est;*[82] perhaps you forget that his heart identified itself with the Sacred Heart of Jesus, *Cor itaque Christi erat cor Pauli;*[83] on the other hand God, who knows what is within you, sees through the thin veneer of a superficial religiosity everything that burdens your conscience again and again, that whole hidden infidelity, all those misuses of grace and this sort of progressive paralysis of your spiritual life, *habentes speciem quidem pietatis, virtutem autem ejus abnegantes.*[84]

And yet it was not always this way! You spent the first months of your priestly ministry zealously, vigilantly, in recollection: *Currebatis bene...; quis vos fascinavit non obedire veritati?*[85]

---

[76] "For I tell you, that unless your justice abound more than that of the scribes and Pharisees, you shall not enter into the kingdom of heaven" (Mt. 5:20).

[77] Preaching and evangelizing" (Lk. 8:1).

[78] Cf. Jn. 4:34.

[79] "He passed the whole night in the prayer of God" (Lk. 6:12).

[80] "My daily instance, the solicitude for all the churches" (2Cor. 11:28).

[81] "I have laboured more abundantly than all they" (1Cor. 15:10).

[82] "For to me, to live is Christ" (Phil. 1:21).

[83] "Paul's heart was Christ's Heart" (St. John Chrysostom, *Homilia 32 in epistolam ad Romanos,* 3; PG (Latin text) 32, 680).

[84] "Having an appearance indeed of godliness but denying the power thereof" (2Tim. 3:5).

[85] "You did run well.... Who hath bewitched you that you should not obey the truth?" (Gal. 5:7; 3:1).

Salus Tua Ego Sum[86]

Oh! At least now, once and for all, stop hurrying down that disastrous, precipitous path; step aside from the "broad way that leadeth to destruction".[87] Seriously examine the state of your soul; and although "you were heretofore darkness," now without delay become "light in the Lord".[88]

Multum facit qui multum diligit,[89] says the author of *The Imitation of Christ.* St. Paul wrote in fear and trembling a sentence that sounds like the Apostle's repudiation of the distracted life: *Ne forte, cum aliis praedicaverim, ipse reprobus efficiar.*[90] Stop, I beseech you, by all that is dearest to you: *Obsecro vos per mansuetudinem et modestiam Christi!*[91] Jesus, who has been banished from your thoughts and from the stirrings of your heart—for in reality that is what this is all about—Jesus looks at you and shivers, and His divine lips murmur the old prayer: *Pater, dimitte illis, non enim sciunt quid faciunt.*[92]

Yes, allow me to make my own the merciless anathema of St. Bernard: "Cursed be all business that keeps us from becoming better every day."[93]

Starting today, adopt again the habit of a well-founded, sincere, constant, well-ordered piety, from which you have unwisely turned away..., *deliciosa ad saporem, solida ad nutrimentum, efficax ad medicinam.*[94] This is a right and a duty, a sacred right and a sacred

---

[86] I am your salvation.

[87] Cf. Mt. 7:13.

[88] Eph. 5:8.

[89] "He who love much does much" (Thomas à Kempis, *The Imitation of Christ,* Book I, Chapter 15).

[90] "Lest perhaps when I have preached to others, I myself should become a castaway" (1Cor. 9:27).

[91] "I beseech you, by the mildness and modesty of Christ" (2Cor. 10:1).

[92] "Father, forgive them, for they know not what they do" (Lk. 23:34).

[93] The saint made so bold as to classify the government of the entire Church among the accursed works, insofar as it occupied all the activity of the Supreme Shepherd and kept him from the practices of the interior life.

[94] "Delicious in taste, solidly nourishing, and an effective remedy" (St. Bernard of Clairvaux, *Sermo LXVII in Cantica Canticorum: De mirabili affectu dilectionis sponsae, quem eructat propter amorem Christi sponsi,* 1; PL 183, 1102).

duty; "Put on Christ, the gentle Christ."[95] You would strive in vain to spread the kingdom of God in souls, if the Lord were not in the first place the absolute Master of your own soul, for "You cannot be of help to others unless you have first devoted yourself to the reform of your own life."[96] The saints who devoted themselves the most to the exterior life often returned to the cell of their heart; or better, they never entirely left it; and since they always lived in the light of God, their soul rested on the firm ground of meditation and love despite the unavoidable storms. *Amans Deum anima, sub Deo despicit universa.*[97]

When it is separated from an overflowing reserve of well-founded piety and intensive supernatural life, exterior action melts away into useless noise, a magnificent soap bubble—you can see this sad comedy every day. What is human becomes inflated without the divine things that build up.[98] This is naturalism in the apostolate, *discipulus supra Magistrum;*[99] and so the cup from the holy temple is defiled all too often at Baltassar's banquet.

Close this book for a moment and reflect in silence about the serious words—which are every beautiful and ever new—of somebody who understands something about the duties and dangers of pastoral ministry: *Si linguis hominum loquar et angelorum..., et si habuero prophetiam et noverim mysteria omnia et omnem scientiam, et si habuero omnem fidem, ita ut montes transferam..., et si distribuero in cibos pauperum omnes facultates meas, et si tradidero corpus meum ita ut ardeam, charitatem autem non habuero,* NIHIL MIHI PRODEST.[100]

---

[95] An expression of St. Catharine of Siena.

[96] St. Margaret Mary, I, 90; II, 410.

[97] "The soul that loves God despises everything that is beneath God" (Thomas à Kempis, *The Imitation of Christ,* Book II, Chapter 5).

[98] "Knowledge puffeth up: but charity edifieth" (1Cor. 8:1).

[99] "The disciple [is not] above his master" (Lk. 6:40).

[100] "If I speak with the tongues of men and of angels... and if I should have prophecy and should know all mysteries and all knowledge, and if I should have all faith, so that I could remove mountains.... And if I should distribute all my goods to feed the poor, and if I should deliver my body to be burned, and have not charity, it profiteth me nothing" (1Cor. 13:1-3). Louis-Claude Fillion, *La sainte Bible commentée d'après la Vulgate et les textes originaux* [The Holy Bible, with a commentary based on the Vulgate and the original texts], 8 vols. (Paris: Letouzey et Ané, 1903-1905), 8:185 noted: "This is one of the most beautiful pages that have ever been written

Oh yes, I sincerely wish you this: *Deus... det vobis spiritum sapientiae et revelationis, in agnitione ejus, illuminatos oculos cordis vestri.*[101] And since Jesus invites us to this, all of us need to return, once for all, to His Sacred Heart: *Ad Cor reclusum vulnere, ad mite Cor accedite.*[102] Only at this glowing hearth of love can we satisfy our soul, which hungers for the infinite; only in this abyss of all virtues, in this eternal source of perfection can we renew our strength, which has been exhausted or weakened by long fasting; only in this paradise of bliss, *fons totius consolationis,*[103] do we find the necessary strength and the ardor with which to smile again at life, which is so divinely beautiful, with its pains and its tears, if one loves Jesus, if one believes in love!

Meanwhile there is no time to lose! *Nescit tarda molimina spiritus sancti gratia.*[104] "Woe to the souls that are covered with dirt and consumed with thirst beside the spring of living water, for they will never again be cleansed or slaked!"[105] Of course the performance of exterior service is not being berated, but rather the abuse of it; here are the thoughts of St. Margaret Mary: "Do not think that the reasonable work for the salvation of souls that He has entrusted to your care is an obstacle to the salvation of your own soul; on the contrary, through this means you oblige God's goodness to grant you great assistance, so as to achieve it with less danger."[106] Moreover the same saint wrote: "A heart that seeks God alone finds Him everywhere."[107]

---

in human language. One cannot add any commentary to such words; one reads them in adoration and love."

[101] "That God ... may give unto you the spirit of wisdom and of revelation, in the knowledge of him: the eyes of your heart enlightened" (Eph. 1:17-18).

[102] "To the Heart opened by the wound, come to this meek and lowly Heart" (Matins and Vespers hymn, *Quicumque certum quaeritis* from the Office of the Sacred Heart of Jesus from the year 1786, when the Office had not yet been prescribed for the universal Church).

[103] Source of all consolation (Litany of the Sacred Heart).

[104] "The grace of the Holy Ghost does not recognize tardy efforts" (St. Ambrose, *Expositio Evangelii secundum Lucam* 1:39-40, II, 19; PL 15, 1560).

[105] St. Margaret Mary, I, 105; II, 144.

[106] St. Margaret Mary, II, 366.

[107] St. Margaret Mary, II, 686.

Si Scires Donum Dei[108]

Young minister of the sanctuary, why do you hesitate so much to be convinced by the logic of love? Do you want to leave yourself open to the Divine Master's accusation: *Qui ex Deo est, verba Dei audit; propterea vos non auditis, quia ex Deo non estis?*[109] What then are you looking for so eagerly besides Him? What attracts you more?

Knowledge? But "in the ocean of the Heart of Jesus"[110] "all treasures of wisdom and knowledge [of God]"[111] are hidden and united! Have you not grasped this? *Bonum quod amas, ab ipso est.*[112]

What else motivates you? A thirst for souls? But He is "rich unto all that call upon Him"[113], He is all heart, He is love itself, He is by right, as well as in fact, "King and center of all hearts" (Litany of the Sacred Heart).

Are there rebellious sinners who thwart all careful efforts, who until yesterday, or even today, have rejected all the invitations of grace? Yet He became the sacrificial Lamb for them too; He is "the propitiation for the sins of the whole world",[114] He is "patient and rich in mercy"[115], He is "the resurrection and the life".[116]

Are there sick people whose thoughts about sins committed long ago or just recently are embittering the last days of their life? The Heart of Jesus is the salvation of all who hope in Him; He is the *comfort of the dying* (Litany of the Sacred Heart), in Him there is "plenteous redemption" (Ps. 129); He is the inexhaustible *source of life and holiness* (Litany of the Sacred Heart); in Him and through Him, *solatium animae et vera cordis laetitia*,[117] we find the grace of

---

[108] "If thou didst know the gift of God" (Jn. 4:10).

[109] "He that is of God heareth the words of God. Therefore you hear them not, because you are not of God" (Jn. 8:47).

[110] St. Margaret Mary, II, 405.

[111] Cf. Col. 2:3.

[112] "The good that you love comes from Him" (St. Augustine, *The Confessions*, IV, 12).

[113] Rom. 10:12.

[114] Cf. 1 Jn. 2:2.

[115] Joel 2:13.

[116] Jn. 11:25.

[117] The soul's consolation and the heart's true gladness" (Thomas à Kempis, *The Imitation of Christ*, Book II, Chapter 5).

God, and consequently life everlasting.[118] Are you convinced of this? *Quodcumque bonum cupis, quodcumque pulchrum quaeris, ... totum in Ipso invenies.*[119]

In your name St. Paul wrote: *Nos autem sensum Christi habemus!*[120]

Oh, if only it were so! How we would treasure heavenly things then! How we would then feel united to the teacher of truth, so as to become all-powerful with Him! If we really know the mind of Christ, why does it remain for so many of us a dead letter, as does the momentous saying of St. John of the Cross: "The slightest act of pure love has in God's eyes more value for the Church and for oneself than all other works taken together."[121]

The Holy Ghost beseeches us with ineffable sighs to perform our duty: *Bonus eris minister Christi Jesu.*[122] What right do we have then to be content to live like strangers with respect to this source of infinite love, which we are supposed to help gain dominion over the world? Why do we continue to reject as dreamy mysticism the saying of St. Peter Julien Eymard: "One single act of love that remains in the soul is for Jesus more glorious than all the apostolate throughout the world."[123]

Do we not know, then, that the adorable Heart of the Redeemer is the most perfect creature, *stella splendida et matutina*?[124] Is it necessary, right in the middle of Christendom, to repeat that this Heart is the *pretiosa margarita*[125] of the Gospel, the most sublime ideal of all beauty, the constant source of all graces, the seat of all joy, the mystery of all holiness, the ultimate reason for and

---

[118] Cf. Rom 6:23.

[119] "Whatever good you desire, whatever beauty you seek, ... you will find it all in Him (St. Bernard of Clairvaux, *Sermo de humana misericordia, inter opusculos,* PL 184, 1113).

[120] "We have the mind of Christ" (1 Cor. 2:16).

[121] *The Spiritual Canticle* (OCD Publications), GT181. Note on the following (29th) stanza.

[122] "Thou shalt be a good minister of Christ Jesus" (1 Tim. 4:6).

[123] This sentence is an excerpt from the spiritual diary of the saint (who was canonized on December 9, 1962, by Pope John XXIII). Obviously it contrasts an act of interior love with exterior works which lack love or that are accompanied only by a very weak, imperfect love.

[124] "The bright and morning star" (cf. Apoc. 22:16; Num. 24:17).

[125] "Pearl of great price" (Mt. 13:46).

the most effective instrument of any apostolate, the marvel of the angels, the bliss of the saints, the charm of creation? Do we not know that the heavenly spirits and the souls of the blessed spend their whole eternity enraptured by the ineffable vision of the Most Sacred Heart, *Speculum sine macula Dei majestatis et imago bonitatis illius?*[126] How is it that this Sacred Heart, *totus desiderabilis*,[127] this Heart so meek, which makes Paradise drunk with bliss, *quia ipse est Sanctorum aeterna requies*,[128] seems so dull and insipid to some of His priests? If we are really guided by the welfare of souls, then why do we seek the remedy for the evil of this unfortunate society where it cannot be found, and why do we forget the one infallible, salutary medicine, without which all others can accomplish nothing, namely the Catholic devotion to the Most Sacred Heart of Jesus?

There might be some justified excuse for our mistrust, our hesitation, if this were a pious, human invention; but no, Jesus Himself revealed it to us. It is an invitation of His love: *Si non locutus fuissem eis*, He might say in reference to us, *peccatum non haberent.*[129] Let us therefore not oppose the weight of His divine authority with our petty excuses or empty prejudices. Rather, let us adore the purposes of the Lord reverently and let us put His instructions into practice willingly. Let us give Jesus to souls so as to give souls to Jesus: *Haec est autem vita aeterna ut cognoscant te solum Deum verum, et quem misisti Jesum Christum.*[130] For—and we must take this for granted—only the Sacred Heart of Jesus can effectively enlighten minds that suffer from the continual darkness of skepticism; He alone, "the Man of sorrows",[131] will strengthen the will that has been weakened

---

[126] "The unspotted mirror of God's majesty, and the image of his goodness" (Wis. 7:26).

[127] "All lovely" (Cant. 5:16).

[128] "For He is the eternal rest of the saints" (Thomas à Kempis, *The Imitation of Christ,* Book III, Chapter 21).

[129] "If I had not come and spoken to them, they would not have sin" (Jn. 15:22).

[130] "Now this is eternal life: That they may know thee, the only true God, and Jesus Christ, whom thou hast sent" (Jn. 17:3).

[131] Isa. 53:3.

by the fever of pleasure; He alone, the "Prince of peace",[132] can pacify the class hatred and silence the hidden antagonism that divides peoples and nations and threatens to destroy the peace of mankind once again in the near future; "for a very special effect of this devotion is to reunite divided hearts and to bring peace to souls."[133]

Videte Vocationem Vestram[134]

What? You still doubt? How long? You, of all people, who are supposed to teach others, will not do yourself what Jesus demands of them? ... And yet—tell me in all simplicity—perhaps you do so out of ignorance. Then excuse me for wondering: *Tu es magister in Israel et haec ignoras?* [135]

And yet the Spirit of the Lord descended upon your head, and your hands were anointed with the Holy Chrism; upon you was conferred the authority to bind and loose, to preach and consecrate, all this in Christ's name: *In omnibus divites facti estis in illo, in omni verbo et in omni scientia.*[136] And this has been the case for five, ten, maybe twenty years, *tanto tempore vobiscum sum, et non cognovistis me*??[137] Remember: in the Name of Jesus Christ you received the imposition of hands; you are a priest *in aeternum* [for ever] only to promote His honor and to work for His glorification. Think of that now and then: *Admoneo te ut ressuscites gratiam Dei, quae est in te.*[138] On the solemn day of your priestly ordination you were dubbed a *knight of the Sacred Heart of Jesus*. Since that happy moment you have represented Jesus; therefore you must defend His rights and faithfully imitate His virtues, promote His honor always and everywhere, *collaudare, benedicere et praedicare.*[139] Does His Blood

---

[132] Isa. 9:6.

[133] Margaret Mary, II, 557.

[134] "See your vocation" (1Cor. 1:26).

[135] "Art thou a master in Israel, and knowest not these things?" (Jn. 3:10).

[136] "In all things you are made rich in him, in all utterance and in all knowledge (1Cor. 1:5).

[137] "Have I been so long a time with you and have you not known me?" (Jn. 14:9).

[138] "For which cause I admonish thee that thou stir up the grace of God which is in thee" (2Tim. 1:6).

[139] "Praise, bless and proclaim" (Preface in honor of the Most Blessed Virgin Mary).

not flow in all your veins? Are you not fed with His spotless Flesh? "Now you should no longer live, but He in you!"[140]

Be meek, humble, patient; be kind; be chaste as He is, *aptus ad amandum, fortis ad patiendum, stabilis ad perseverandum.*[141] You are placed on the lamp stand in order to shine and illuminate; without embarrassment you must be able to tell the faithful: *Imitatores mei estote, sicut et ego Christi.*[142]

Think about, I beg you: When you absolve sins, when you consecrate, when you cleanse and implore, be mindful of your dignity; think of it with heartfelt gratitude and infinite meekness, instead of meanly regretting what you are not longer permitted to desire; prepare to ascend, willingly and enthusiastically to climb the sun-drenched mountain tops to which the ineffable grace of your priesthood calls and leads you: *Videte vocationem vestram.*[143]

Purity and Love

No doubt about it: On account of painful separations and the loneliness that is necessarily connected with ecclesiastical celibacy—a very wise law of renunciation and self-denial—a profound emptiness that is difficult to describe very quickly forms in the heart of a young Levite, which can be filled only by an immeasurable love, as experience shows. Many an observer has been tempted to pity the Catholic clergy and to ask foolishly, "Why should a Catholic priest be forbidden to love?"

Forbidden to love? If such nonsense were the case, then we would all have to rise up as one man—we priests first of all—and condemn this horrible tyranny; we would have to rebel against priestly chastity as the most useless, most senseless and most inhumane of all sacrifices. Nature itself gives us the right to love, and if that is not enough, it imposes on us the gentle duty of love. Woe to him who tramples this universal law; woe to him who reviles this unavoidable need of the heart!

---

[140] Cf. Gal. 2:20: "I live, now not I, but Christ liveth in me."

[141] "Fit to love, courageous to suffer, and constant to persevere" (Thomas à Kempis, *The Imitation of Christ*, Book III, Chapter 5).

[142] "Be ye followers of me, as I also am of Christ" (1Cor. 4:16).

[143] "See your vocation" (1Cor. 1:26).

It is true, the Redeemer wants chaste ministers. He demands that they offer to Him ceaselessly, and to Him alone, an ardent love in a pure heart like a heavenly fragrance in a golden censer. But He wants this because in His divine wisdom He knows that one can preserve perpetual youth only when one successfully preserves perpetual purity; that the human heart—even though it may be free from any other earthly attachment—is always too narrow to accept a "love that knows no limits". Holy Church, which is a mother, after receiving at the foot of the altar the ordinand's voluntary, perpetual and formal renunciation of ever joining with another weak, imperfect creature, wishes to become the priest's bride. As a precious dowry for this mystical marriage she brings him all the radiant glory of her twenty centuries, all the shining examples of her saints, her spotless history, woven out of good deeds and triumphs. To the priest who promises her eternal fidelity, she entrusts with great emotion the long line of the suffering, to be consoled, the countless host of her little ones and the afflicted, who are to be guarded and defended, a whole army of sinners, so that he can lead them back to God with tender love.

And you are still trying to tell me that the priest is forbidden to love? Tell instead the slanderers of our reputation that no one in the world has a greater right and duty to love than the priest, because for him love coincides with a sublime vocation, which in turn is sealed with the most sacred oath, and that for him every step along the path of love is necessarily a step forward on the path of holiness.

St. Ambrose defines the priest as follows: *Vicarius amoris Christi*,[144] the viceroy or representative of the love that dwells in the Sacred Heart of Jesus. The priest is therefore not, as some very foolishly maintain, a slave who drags his humiliating chain along with him and curses it. Rather, he is a great, free and strong being who is supposed to live on love, freedom, joy and holiness, *superabundo gaudio in omni tribulatione*.[145]

Someone will object that this all-embracing love, which in a certain sense is imposed, is necessarily superficial, that it does

---

[144] Cf. *Expositio Evangelii secundum Lucam*, X, 175; PL 15, 1848; St. Ambrose, commenting on Jn. 21:17, says about St. Peter: *Amoris sui nobis velut vicarium relinquebat (Dominus)* ["The Lord left him to us as the representative of His love"], a saying that writers have extended to all priests.
[145] "I exceedingly abound with joy in all our tribulation" (2Cor. 7:4).

not satisfy the longing of the heart that strives for intimacy and affection and wishes to pour itself out in a freely chosen friendship. *Sine amico*, says *The Imitation of Christ, non potes bene vivere.*[146] I know it very well, you are partly right; but do you perhaps suppose that God did not make provisions for that, since we have such a need for someone who understands us, who brings us relief and comforts us? I am not speaking about human friends, who are not all that rare; I am speaking above all about the divine Friend whose Heart lives in the tabernacle and who shares in our human nature without the slightest imperfection in His sympathy. *Iste Sponsus non modo amans, sed amor est.*[147]

From this grows, as you see, a mutual, justified and providential relationship, which demands a fusion of hearts, the Heart of Jesus with the heart of the priest: *Qui diligit me..., et ego diligam eum...: sicut dilexit me Pater, et ego dilexi vos.*[148]

To be robbed of our friendship would be extremely bitter for Jesus! Listen to how affectionately He speaks to us: *Vos amici mei estis..., vos dixi amicos.*[149] Therefore He wants us to be His friends forever, friends who are one heart and one soul with Him, so as to be conformed to Him, so that we might be worthy and capable of continuing His mission of love effectively. Moreover, "since the One who loves us is all-powerful, let us therefore love and no longer shall anything seem difficult to us."[150]

Do you not see that this friendship is the foundation of your moral greatness, the ultimate reason for your chastity?

Consequently let us foster among us a profound respect for this angelic virtue, which is so neglected, so reviled and so desecrated.

---

[146] "Without a friend thou canst not well live" (Thomas à Kempis, *The Imitation of Christ*, Book II, Chapter 8).

[147] "This Bridegroom is not only a lover, but is love" (St. Bernard of Clairvaux, *Sermo LXXXIII in Cantica Canticorum: Qualiter anima, quantumcunque vitiis corrupta, adhuc per amorem castum et sanctum potest redire ad similtudinem sponsi, id est Christi* [How the soul, however corrupted by vices, can still return by chaste and holy love to a likeness to her Spouse, Christ], 4; PL 183, 1183).

[148] "He that loveth me... I will love him.... As the Father hath loves me, I also have loved you" (Jn. 14:21; 15:9).

[149] "You are my friends.... I have called you friends" (Jn. 15:14-15).

[150] St. Margaret Mary, II, 292.

Let us strive to make it shine radiantly from our person and from our life, as the whiteness of the Sacred Host in the monstrance shines; and let us seek in humility, which is "purity of spirit", the mystery of continence, which is "humility of the flesh": *Fiat, Domine, cor meum et corpus meum immaculatum, ut non confundar.*[151]

The Secret of Success

Oh, if only you would think about this seriously, priest of Jesus Christ; if only you were humbler and more docile! If only you believed in love, *si scires donum Dei!*[152] You know what the Apostle desires: It is a statement of fact and at the same time an invitation: *In medio nationis pravae et perversae ... lucetis, sicut luminaria in mundo.*[153] But where do you find this shining light, which must radiate from your person in order to enlighten mankind? Nowhere else but in the Heart of Jesus, "the life of our souls and the love of our hearts".[154] *Ego sum lux mundi. Qui sequitur me ... habebit lumen vitae.*[155]

Your mission is to cause the light of truth to shine with fearless faith, to preach a gospel of sacrifice and purity to all the unfortunate souls who no longer see and no longer want to see, who languish in darkness and in the shadow of death, who are plunged into a terrible dark night of the soul and have become enemies of the cross of Christ, *quorum deus venter est.*[156]

There are hundreds, maybe thousands of souls for whom you have been appointed the legitimate shepherd and who treat you— as you well know—with indifference and contempt. They have only hatred, slander and injustice to repay you for your care, and they make you drink with Jesus the cup of His passion. Poor lost

---

[151] "Lord, may my heart and my body remain spotless, and then I will not be put to shame" (*Breviarium Romanum*, Feast of St. Cecilia, Matins, 1st Responsorium).
[152] "If thou didst know the gift of God" (Jn. 4:10).
[153] "In the midst of a crooked and perverse generation... you shine as lights in the world" (Phil. 2:15).
[154] St. Margaret Mary, II, 163.
[155] "I am the light of the world. He that followeth me ... shall have the light of life" (Jn. 8:12).
[156] "Whose God is their belly" (Phil. 3:19).

sheep, led astray by the world's vanity, tyrannized by their hunger for money, exhausted by feverish desires and pleasures, fooled by the deceptive promises of freedom, like those about which St. Paul says: *eratis sine Christo ... et sine Deo in hoc mundo.*[157] How fitting it is to be concerned about their unfortunate lot! And despite everything you can rescue them, if only you are willing!

You reply that a thousand attempts have led nowhere, that your long prayers and your pious efforts in your pastoral experience have produced no results... *per totam noctem laborantes, nihil coepimus.*[158]

Would you like me, then, to tell you a secret of how to lead them back to the truth? *Noli timere, tantummodo crede.*[159] If they do not pay attention to you, if they do not love you, if they do not want to hear you, if they ridicule you and Him whom you represent, if they do not want to come to Jesus, ... bring Jesus to them, commend them with all your zeal to His Sacred Heart and if you can, then speak to them about this Most Sacred Heart, *omni voluptate dulcior, ... omni luce clarior, ... omni honore sublimior.*[160] This last condition, you understand very well, is indispensable: *Quomodo ... invocabunt, in quem non crediderunt? Aut quomodo credent ei, quem non audierunt? Quomodo Autem Audient Sine Praedicante?*[161]

Moreover "it is enough to do the possible things that He prompts us to do. Once we have scattered the seed, we must let the grace of this divine Heart work, which takes care to tend the seed and to make it bear fruit through the anointing of Its ardent love."[162]

Meanwhile believe, believe firmly that ignorance of the Heart of Jesus is the reason for all these evils of our age. This is the ultimate

---

[157] "You were ... without Christ ... and without God in this world" (Eph. 2:12).

[158] "We have laboured all the night and have taken [i.e. caught] nothing" (Lk 5:5).

[159] "Fear not, only believe" (Mk. 5:36).

[160] "Sweeter than any pleasure, ... brighter than any light, ... more exalted than any honor" (St. Augustine, *Confessions*, Book IX, Chapter 1; PL 32, 763).

[161] "How then shall they call on him in whom they have not believed? Or how shall they believe him of whom they have not heard? And how shall they hear without a preacher?" (Rom. 10:14).

[162] St. Margaret Mary, II, 585.

reason for this sworn hatred against the priest, a hatred that causes such serious damage to justice and to history: *Propter hoc mundus non novit nos, quia non novit eum.*[163]

St. Paul of the Cross, whose knowledge of souls was profound, used to say that love alone can make our *generatio mala et adultera*[164] open to faith. I repeat it to you in his own words: "Sophistry has perverted the mind of man to such an extent that the only thing left for us to do is to speak to the heart." But who could speak more and better to the heart of man than the heart of a God? "Oh, how fitting are His mercies upon so many ungrateful, unbelieving hearts, which without them would perish."[165] And why such a wealth of revelations in Paray-le-Monial? Why so many loving invitations, so many signs of hope for redemption? *Ut vitam habeant, et abundantius habeant!*[166]

Now open the Sacred Scriptures and read: *Quos dedisti mihi, non perdidi ex eis quemquam.*[167] What an exalted ideal for an apostolic heart! To lead to heaven all the souls entrusted to him! My God, would it be possible? Really all of them?

This is the Lord's secret. Meanwhile let us not forget: Even if this triumph of grace is possible, it still remains a jealously guarded prerogative, which is reserved to the friends of the Heart of Jesus: "My divine Savior assured me that those who labor for the salvation of souls will have *the art of touching the hardest hearts* and will obtain *marvelous success*, if they themselves are animated with a tender devotion to His Divine Heart, if they strive to lead others to this devotion and to establish it everywhere, ... and if they draw all their light from this source."[168]

To convert souls is the holy desire of an apostle. *Nam et otiosus est sermo docentis, si praebere non valet incendium amoris.*[169]

---

[163] "Therefore the world knoweth not us, because it knew not him" (1Jn. 3:1).

[164] "Evil and adulterous generation" (Mt. 12:39).

[165] St. Margaret Mary, II, 346.

[166] "That they may have life and may have it more abundantly" (Jn. 10:10).

[167] "Those whom thou gavest me have I kept: and none of them is lost" (Jn. 17:12).

[168] St. Margaret Mary, II, 407, 439, 628.

[169] "For the preaching of a teacher is in vain, unless it is capable of communicating the fire of love" (St. Gregory the Great, *Homilia XXX in Evangelia: Habita ad populum in basilica sancti Petri apostoli die sancto Pentecostae*

Many proclaim the Gospel in God's Church, but apostles are rare! *Nam si decem millia paedagogorum habeatis in Christo, sed non multos patres.*[170]

Outstanding knowledge of theology and philosophy, of sacred and secular sciences, a command of rhetorical skills, the art of pleasing a select audience and winning its agreement and applause, to call one's own a noble and dignified bearing, broad and solemn gestures, a harmonious, flattering voice, an elegant style that enraptures minds with vivid, sensitive descriptions, exquisite comparisons and appropriate quotations; the ability to hold the listeners' attention by well-constructed, euphonious sentences, by a wealth of sublime thoughts; the ability to present beautiful new things, to be able to apply the treasures of doctrine, to be a master in analyzing and synthesizing events, to have the difficult art of controlling the masses; to exert a mysterious, moving and captivating fascination on rebellious minds without contradicting them... what invaluable talents! But unfortunately, these are only natural weapons and consequently they bear little fruit. *Nonne stultam fecit Deus, sapientiam hujus mundi?*[171] These are paltry, human means, and even assuming that they were all to be found together in a priest, they would produce in him the dangerous illusion of *being a superman*; in practice they would not suffice to save one single soul, much less a whole nation. *Tantum qui amore ardent, ceteros inflammare sciunt.*[172] You know very well that justification is a work of the supernatural order. *Voluntatem a peccato in bonum mutari, non contingit nisi per gratiam Dei,*[173] the Angelic Doctor teaches. That is why so many

---

[Jn. 14:23-31), II, 5; PL 76, 1223).

[170] "For if you have ten thousand instructors in Christ, yet not many fathers" (1Cor. 4:15).

[171] "Hath not God made foolish the wisdom of this world?" (1Cor. 1:20). St. Thomas Aquinas said: *Melior est amor Dei quam cognitio* ["The love of God is better than knowledge of God"] (Summa Theologiae I, q. 82, art. 3 corp.), and St. John wrote: *Qui non diligit non novit Deum, quoniam Deus charitas est* ["He that loveth not knoweth not God: for God is charity"] (1 Jn. 4:8).

[172] "Only those who glow with love themselves know how to set on fire the hearts of others" (Benedict XV, Encyclical *Humani Generis*, 15 June 1917).

[173] "To turn the will from sin to the good is achieved solely through God's grace alone" (St. Thomas Aquinas, *Summa Contra Gentiles*, IV, 93).

of us exhaust ourselves with calls to penance throughout Lent, speaking to a select audience, and at the end very few of the listeners change their lives. Speakers who are applauded like to accuse the evil of the age...; in reality it is all too often their own fault: *Voluntes esse legis doctores..., conversi sunt in vaniloquium.*[174]

In order to convert souls and lead them to God, eloquence, as theological treatises teach us, is in itself not enough: *non in sapientia verbi, ut non evacuetur crux Christi.*[175] What is needed is an art that is certainly not learned in the schools nor in publications with learned treatises, namely the art of communicating divine things, the holy unction that penetrates with grace into the innermost recesses of the conscience so as "to root up... and to destroy, and to build and to plant".[176] And this blessed art, the secret key to which is given to us by our vocation, is drawn directly and exclusively from the adorable Heart of Him who is set up as teacher of the truth, *coepit facere et docere.*[177]

Oh, we have had enough of this "knowledge that puffs up" and that comes from Christian professorships; we need instead the "charity [that] edifies".[178] And if so much apostolic toil has remained fruitless until now, *prophetae fuerunt in ventum locuti,*[179] then let us hastily return to the Heart of Jesus, to this ineffable dwelling place of infinite love, so as to learn from him, the *magister magistrorum,*[180] the secret of converting hearts; from Him alone, for He alone has promised it: *cathedram in caelo habet, qui corda docet.*[181]

You, who toil all day searching for the little sheep that has gone astray, you who weep like Jeremias over the empty, profaned

---

[174] "Desiring to be teachers of the law... they are turned aside unto vain babbling" (1Tim. 1:6-7).

[175] "Not in wisdom of speech, lest the cross of Christ should be made void" (1Cor. 1:17).

[176] Jer. 1:10.

[177] "Jesus began to do and to teach" (Acts 1:1).

[178] 1Cor. 8:1.

[179] "The prophets have spoken in the wind" (Jer 5:13).

[180] "Teacher of all teachers" (Thomas à Kempis, *The Imitation of Christ,* Book III, Chapter 43).

[181] "He who instructs hearts has a teacher's chair in heaven" (St. Augustine, *In epistolam Ioannis ad Parthos, tractatus* III [1 Jn. 2:18-27], 2, 13; PL 35, 2004).

sheepfold, you who "wait with silence for the salvation of God",[182] you whose eardrums has been shattered by the demonic cry of the enraged crowd: *Nolumus hunc regnare super nos,*[183] come and rest at least occasionally on this gentle Heart of the teacher: *Bonus est Dominus sperantibus in eum, animae quaerenti illum.*[184] Come without fear, with trust and humility, and keep in mind that apart from him you will find only darkness and sin, illusions and lies, *non est in alio aliquo salus.*[185] He is the one Shepherd: *Ego sum pastor bonus.*[186] Even when you sleep, His Heart keeps watch; be therefore a shepherd with Him, and the sheep will recognize His voice in your voice and follow you: *Ubi illius inspiratio et unctio non est, forinsecus inaniter perstrepunt verba.*[187]

In simplicity of heart go to His school, listen piously to His instructions, and first put into practice what you are supposed to teach others. Ponder in pious meditations the mysteries of this Heart that has loved mankind so much, learn from Him the *pedagogy of love*, and then run, fly everywhere the Spirit of the Lord invites you, to every place to which your ministry calls you, wherever souls to be saved await you. He will go before you with His grace, He will protect you like a shield, he will care for you as the "apple of His eye";[188] He is always with you, and you can repeat about Him what He Himself says about His Father: *Qui me misit mecum est, et non reliquit me solum, quia quae placita sunt ei facio semper.*[189]

Be an apostle who is convinced of this devotion, and you will see! ... As though by some mysterious magic you will see the ice of religious indifference melt away; you will see how the dark clouds of error dissipate; you will see how the most barren trees are covered

---

[182] Lam. 3:26.

[183] "We will not have this man to reign over us" (Lk. 19:14).

[184] "The Lord is good to them that hope in him, to the soul that seeketh him" (Lam. 3:25).

[185] "Neither is there salvation in any other" (Acts 4:12).

[186] "I am the good shepherd" (Jn. 10:14).

[187] "Where His inspiration and unction are not present, words resound abroad in vain" (St. Augustine, *In epistolam Ioannis ad Parthos, tractatus* III [1 Jn. 2:18-27], 2, 13; PL 35, 2004).

[188] Ps. 16:8.

[189] "And he that sent me is with me: and he hath not left me alone. For I do always the things that please him" (Jn. 8:29).

with fruit; you will see how mountains are moved from one place to another and how a stream of new life flows in the dried-up veins of this spoiled society that is beset by doubts. Believe—Jesus assures you—that "the principal purpose of this devotion is to convert souls to His love."[190]

Believe "that He will be the teacher of the hearts which He desires to possess."[191] St. Madeleine Sophie Barat used to tell her spiritual daughters: "You must constantly take refuge in this source of life.... You get the impression that in these very sad times the Most Holy Trinity allows Itself to be prevailed upon only in the name of the adorable Heart of Jesus."[192]

You, who sigh under the burden of great trials and find no consolation in your desolate soul, know that there is a means, indeed an infallible method, of making peace and reaching the goal: devotion to this Heart, "which knows our weaknesses"[193] and "is the altar of our sacrifices".[194]

Et haec scribimus vobis ut gaudeatis, et gaudium vestrum sit plenum.[195]

Unfounded Hostility

Someone told me—a priest said it, actually—that "honoring the Sacred Heart is a *paltry, sentimental devotion.*" One is really tempted to think of the words of St. Jude Thaddaeus: *Quaecumque quidem ignorant, blasphemant.*[196]

It is as clear as day, however, that sentimentality has nothing to do with this wonderful expression of Catholic piety, which St. Alphonsus described as the most beautiful and the best-founded

---

[190] St. Margaret Mary, II, 355.

[191] St. Margaret Mary, II, 355.

[192] Mgr. Louis Baunard, *Histoire de la Mère Barat fondatrice de la Société du Sacré-Coeur de Jésus* [Life of Mother Barat, Foundress of the Society of the Sacred Heart of Jesus] (Paris: Librairie Poussièlgue Frères, 1876), II:372-373.

[193] Cf. Isa. 53:3.

[194] St. Margaret Mary, II, 480.

[195] "These things we write to you that you may rejoice and your joy may be full" (1Jn. 1:4).

[196] "These men blaspheme whatever things they know not" (Jude 10).

of all devotions.[197] Our Lord Himself, who is certainly qualified to speak on the subject, explained in definite terms to the "much-beloved pupil of his Sacred Heart"[198] "that He reserved for our age the revelations of His Heart, so as to give men an object and a means that is most excellently suited to move them to love Him, and to love Him valiantly."[199]

Do you understand this? The Sacred Heart of Jesus is nothing other than the effective, living Gospel; it is the Redeemer who has come close to His creatures; it is the revelation of His love, the manifestation of His power; these are promises that have been fulfilled; in a word, it is Jesus, better known and loved. Devotion to the Heart of Jesus is this and nothing more—let us not forget it.

Under the blessed image of this adorable Heart, *verbi Dei sacrarium*,[200] we are invited to contemplate the irresistible attraction of His infinite love, as though in a miniature of our meek and gentle Savior with all His love—"the first of His gifts"[201]—and at the same time with all His good deeds, sufferings, loving gifts, fruits, invitations and yearning.

He is the King of Love, depicted under this symbol, which calls to mind more effectively and more naturally all the virtues, all the tender care and sanctity and the most beautiful, most magnificent and most intimate features of the person of Jesus, and all His words, all His exterior actions inspired by love, without omitting "His mysteries, His joys, His weaknesses, His sacrifices, His priesthood".[202] When we, astonished and deeply moved, contemplate this beaming sun, this masterpiece of the Creator's omnipotence, then we almost necessarily feel awakening

---

[197] "St. Alphonsus says precisely this in the Introduction to his *Novena to the Sacred Heart of Jesus:* The devotion of all devotions is the one that makes us love Jesus Christ.... Now devotion to the Sacred Heart of Jesus is nothing but a spiritual exercise of love for this kindly Savior" (note by the French translator).

[198] St. Margaret Mary, II, 71.

[199] St. Margaret Mary, II, 243.

[200] "Sanctuary of the Word of God" (*Little Office of the Sacred Heart of Jesus,* at None).

[201] Cf. *in ratione doni primi* (St. Thomas Aquinas, *Summa Theologiae* I, q. 38, art. 2, corp.).

[202] Charles Sauvé, *Jésus intime, Dieu intime: Elévations dogmatiques* (Paris: Vic et Amat, 1902; J. De Gigord, 1925), 4 vols., 1:309.

and growing in us a love blended with amazement, gratitude, trust, reparation, atonement, and imitation.... *ut homo non sibi vivat, sed Deo.*[203]

Therefore we should not be surprised that the Sacred Congregation for Rites declared that "The Feast of the Sacred Heart of Jesus is not dedicated to the memory of a particular mystery of His life that had not yet found a place on the liturgical calendar; rather it is the summary of all the other feasts which are individually designed to celebrate one of the mysteries."[204]

The reason for this clarification is obvious: This cult in fact does not call to mind a particular grace but rather lifts our sights to the inexhaustible source of all graces; it does not only celebrate a revelation of God's goodness, but rather the principle and the innermost reason for all the mysteries of Redemption, which had already been accomplished interiorly in the sanctuary of the Sacred Heart of Jesus before it appeared in visible form in the life of the God-man. It is summarized and concentrated in this first act of the most profound, infinite humility, which was the divine response to the *fiat* of the Immaculata.

A beautiful page from the work of a contemporary, well-informed author brings this idea to light splendidly:

> God is love, *Deus caritas est,*[205] and His eternal
> Heart has always loved. Seeking in this eternal love
> of God the reason for the series of all the revealed

---

[203] "That man may live no longer for himself but for God" (St. Thomas Aquinas, *Summa Theologiae*, II-II, q. 17, art. 6, ad 3).

[204] See *Sacra Rituum Congregatio anno 1821 apud Gerdellini, Decreta,* 3:4579. This Decree, it is true, was not included in the new official collection of Decrees, but only because this seemed superfluous, because it is included and supplemented in so very many other Decrees (Bainvel, *Devotion to the Sacred Heart,* Part III, chap. 7, §2; cf. Chapter 1, footnote 26 of this book). Perhaps it is fitting to recall that among all the feasts and commemorations that have been approved by the Church, there is not one that directly and explicitly celebrates the love of Jesus in and of itself; they all have as their object a *mystery of love,* while the cult of the Sacred Heart of Jesus is aimed at celebrating directly and for its own sake the mystery of His love (Terrien, *La dévotion au Sacré-Coeur,* 112; cf. chap. 1, footnote 26 of this book).

[205] 1 Jn. 4:16.

mysteries is the matter of the *theology of the Sacred Heart of Jesus.*

God loves, and to love means to give oneself. He gave us everything: here we have creation.

To love means to speak, so as to communicate oneself to the beloved. God spoke: here we have revelation.

To love means to make oneself similar to the beloved: here we have the Incarnation.

To love means to suffer for the beloved: here we have the Redemption.

To love means to live alongside the beloved: here we have the Eucharist.

To love means to become one with the beloved: here we have Holy Communion.

To love means to rejoice with the beloved: here we have Paradise. *Sic Deus dilexit.*[206]

And since the person of Jesus is a divine person, His created Heart concentrates all the tokens of love of the uncreated Heart of God and summarizes all Its expressions.... It is the living, joyfully throbbing expression of all Catholic mysteries.[207]

Admittedly, under the cloak of this devotion all too many saccharine books and tasteless, blatantly thoughtless brochures have come into circulation, which play on the sickly dispositions of many women who live on sighs and emotions; we find content-free prayers full of useless claims and regrettable illusions, full of historical errors, theological imprecision, obvious contradictions and sprinkled with apocryphal revelations, which ultimately expose the Church's mysticism to ridicule. But these stupid, short-lived works, which spring from a sickly, thoughtless piety (we must say expressly), are a disgrace to this devotion, the opposite of asceticism, a mockery of love. Thank God the Church knows better than to produce the like.

---

[206] "God so loved..." (Jn. 3:16).

[207] Quoted from Mgr. Louis Baunard, *Un siècle de l'Église de France, 1800-1900* [One Century of the Church in France, 1800-1900] (Paris: Poussièlgue, 1901; J. De Gigord, 1922), chapter 10.

Observe sometime this devotion that we are speaking about in the writings of the saints and test its components, study the call to practice it in the Encyclical Letters of the last twenty popes, in the pastoral letters of the most famous bishops; feed your spirit and your heart on the sure doctrine that is drawn from the great works that treat the topic *ex professo* [explicitly]; and then tell me frankly whether you can find anything in God's Church that is more genuine, more manly, greater, more splendid and more in keeping with the Catholic faith; tell me, what other devotion offers greater guarantees of its effectiveness to renew in Christ the society of our day.[208]

Superficial, frivolous minds that consider themselves orthodox have tried to throw this utterly magnificent devotion into the same pot with certain other not-so-serious, even childish devotions that all too easily win the approval of believers who are less bright. They have said repeatedly: "Devotion to the Sacred Heart of Jesus? That is just a fad!"

Our Lord foretold that it would one day be in fashion, and He willed this when He repeated on various occasions that He had reserved it for *the last times.*[209] *It is in fashion*, if you will, because millions of souls throughout the world practice it with the utmost spiritual profit; because it wraps the whole world in an extremely pure atmosphere of zeal and sanctity; *it is in fashion* because it elicits reverence and due affection in all sincere souls. Hundreds of official periodicals, published in thirty different languages, speak about it enthusiastically and with abundant fruits to all classes of believers;[210] essentially, though, it goes back

---

[208] To speak only about the writings of St. Margaret Mary, which constitute a major authority in this field. Especially since the approval granted to them by the Church, we find in them the marks of a strict asceticism that is entirely in harmony with Christ's suffering and sacrifice; this devotion "boasts of Christ's cross, in which are found salvation, life and resurrection". To condemn these writings without having read them is more convenient than honest.

[209] St. Gertrude, *Legatus divinae pietatis* [Messenger of Divine Love], IV, 4; II, 10; St. Margaret Mary, I, 243 and II, 550. The latter saint speaks about the "final centuries". Cf. Bainvel, *Devotion to the Sacred Heart*, Part III, Chapter 1, §3, final note.

[210] Statistics from 1931 showed that issues of *Der Bote des Heiligsten Herzens Jesu* [The Messenger of the Sacred Heart of Jesus], a German monthly magazine of the Apostolate of Prayer, were being published in 40 languages

to the very beginnings of Christianity.[211]

From history it is easy to prove that there have always been believers in the Church who loved the Sacred Heart of Jesus and, in imitation of St. John, regarded it as a prerogative and an excellent honor to be able to rest their weary head and their restless heart on the merciful Heart of the divine teacher. From the beginning and down through the centuries this queen of all devotions remained hidden, as though in an inchoate stage, without any external formalities, without the clarity of theological precision and without practical, ascetical and liturgical applications. Not until a later era did it acquire these features. Yet although it was outwardly absent from Catholic life and had no official, solemn approval by the Church, which alone has the right to declare a private form of devotion legitimate and to make it public— nevertheless who could ever count the generous hearts that were kept separate from the vanities of the world by interior prayer and sacrifice, souls that the Holy Ghost brought to heavenly things and at His prompting gladly contemplated the mysterious source of divine love with a seraphic gaze? Theirs was a lively, deep, powerful and enthusiastic wonder, a tender and moving impulse, a zealous striving, with ardent outbursts, a splendid insight, sweet meditations and true streams of fire, which often received a divine seal in ecstasy and were recorded in lines that were quite

---

for approximately 2.5 million subscribers and were read by 15 million Catholics.

[211] We find a learned treatise about the facts and a wealth of well-selected documents, which withstand all criticism, in the volume by Fr. Auguste Hamon, S.J.: *Histoire de la dévotion au Sacré-Coeur* [History of devotion to the Sacred Heart], 5 vols. (Paris: Gabriel Beauchesne, 1923-1940), vol. 2: *L'aube de la dévotion* [The dawn of the devotion] (Paris, 1925).

In the Middle Ages Germany already revered the Sacred Heart of Jesus, as we do not, through novenas, little offices, ejaculatory prayers and images (cf. Carl Richstätter, *Die Herz-Jesu Verehrung des deutschen Mittelalters* [Paderborn: Bonifacius Druckerei, 1919; Munich: Josef Kösel & Friedrich Pustet, 19242]). For other nations, see the works by Tournier, Thomas, Alet, Baruteil, Paranque, etc.

The writings of St. Gertrude and two other saints named Mechthilde show the intimacy with the Heart of Jesus that these souls had attained. Of course they were especially blessed, but these souls are not at all as rare as one might think, and this was the case long before St. Margaret Mary.

unfairly forgotten. In them we find freshness of feeling, precision of imagery, depth of thought and often theological precision of expression. These are combined with the virginal innocence that is the most magnificent fragrance of sanctity.

"Christianity," Bishop Pie wrote, "can be so perfectly identified with no other devotion than devotion to the Sacred Heart of Jesus."[212]

This beautiful cult grew and was elaborated timidly, so to speak, in the shadow of the medieval cloisters; it finally was revealed, radiant with light and beauty, in the intimacy of Paray-le-Monial and recently had its full and definitive development in the canonization of the humble Visitation Nun. It is a beaming, glorious midday that knows no evening.

A "sentimental" devotion?! A "fashionable" devotion?!

Oh, if only we knew the gift of God better! If only we lived in such a way as to merit a taste of it! *Lingua amoris, ei qui non amat barbara erit.*[213]

If only we understood better the spirit that should animate true devotion to the Sacred Heart of Jesus! If only we were interiorly so disposed, "to live only His life now, to love only with His love now, by surrendering ourselves entirely to Him, so that He might do in us and with us whatever suits His

---

[212] *Lettre synodale à son clergé* [Pastoral Letter to his Clergy], 1857. It is helpful to summarize the theory of this devotion, which has as its object *the person of Jesus,* from the perspective of the most intimate, most beautiful, most attractive feature of this person, namely His love. Devotion to the Cross honors Jesus' sufferings; our devotion honors His love, *i.e.* the loving Jesus. It does not set forth directly the external revelations of this divine love, but rather this divine love, contemplated in itself and symbolized in the image of the Heart, which is the most natural and most effective expression of love. We honor the love that is symbolized in the Heart, and the Heart symbolizes this love. In this way we strive to honor *the whole person of Jesus,* inasmuch as He loves. If Christianity is the religion of love, then it is quite logical and natural for it to be the religion of the Heart of Jesus also!

[213] "The language of love remains alien to the one who does not love" (St. Bernard of Clairvaux, *Sermo LXXIX in Cantica Canticorum: De amore tenaci et indissolubili, quo anima tenet sponsum: item de reditu sponsi in fine saeculi ad Synagogam Judaeorum salvandam,* 1; PL 183, 1163).

good pleasure!"[214] Yes, then we would be convinced that no other devotion demands so much willingness to sacrifice, so much self-denial, so much generosity in doing good, so much purity in life, so much patience with our neighbor, so much ardent zeal in the apostolate. Then we would understand that no other expression of Christian love is capable of producing in a short time such a rich harvest of works of virtue and of spiritual renewal. This is divine love, which gently but at the same time firmly and majestically compels human love and succeeds, as though by means of a holy *inspiration*, in perfectly, constantly and definitively winning the victory over all misery and weakness, over all manifestations of selfishness and sensuality. *Si vis perfectus esse ... veni, sequere me.* [215]

"Let us then love this Sacred Heart, ... this unique love of our souls; ... it is enough to love It to become holy."[216] It transforms our whole interior life and makes it fruitful; it is the indomitable source of renunciation and peace. It is enough to imitate this Heart in order to reinforce our weakness with the strength of Him who overcame the world. With the zealous resolve that He gives to anyone who asks Him for it, every vehement reluctance turns into spiritual joy, and the deadly battle with the flesh turns into ineffable blessedness, because anyone "who has Christ as his spiritual joy"[217] is always calm and at peace, even when his heart is bleeding: *Quasi tristes, semper autem gaudentes.*[218]

Yet even apart from the countless advantages of this blessed devotion, which obtains for us such "treasures of love, mercy, grace, sanctification and salvation"[219]; even if we set aside all the rights of this adorable Heart, which is a "gigantic ocean of countless graces, the starting point and destination of all that is most noble and worthy in the saints,"[220] and look only at the indisputable historical truth of the

---

[214] St. Margaret Mary, II, 330.

[215] "If thou wilt be perfect ... come, follow me" (Mt. 19:21).

[216] St. Margaret Mary, II, 473.

[217] St. Augustine, *Tract. 101 in Evang. Joan.*, 3; PL 35, 1894.

[218] "As sorrowful, yet always rejoicing" (2Cor. 6:10).

[219] St. Margaret Mary, II, 572.

[220] St. John Eudes, *Oeuvres complètes de saint Jean Eudes,* vol. 8, *Le Coeur admirable de la très sacrée Mère de Dieu ou la dévotion au très saint Coeur de la bienheureuse Vierge Marie* [The Admirable Heart of the Most Blessed

revelations of Paray-le-Monial:[221] What would you say about a priest who, when the Eternal High Priest offered His Heart to the world as a miracle of love, as the "last effort of His love",[222] destined "to save many souls from eternal ruin," replied to Him:[223] "I understand none of this, nor do I want to devote myself to the study of this devotion.... I do not know what this cross means, or these thorns, this blood, these flames... nor does that concern me at all"?[224]

Could there be any greater irreverence or folly?

If only this were merely a hypothetical case! But unfortunately it is an historical fact... and an historical fact in our time!

The Sacred Heart of Jesus and the Blessed Sacrament of the Altar

You tell me: "The foundation, center and crown of Catholic piety is the Eucharistic Mystery: this, at least, is an old devotion!"

I agree with you, by all means: "The Most Blessed Sacrament is the *soul of the Church.*"[225] But how can anyone miss the fact, even if he does not review all the similarities that closely connect devotion to the Most Blessed Sacrament and devotion to the Sacred Heart of Jesus with each other, that in the Blessed Sacrament, the mystery of love, the divine Heart, symbol of this love,[226] is really present? On the other hand, according to the

---

Mother of God, or Devotion to the Immaculate Heart of the Blessed Virgin Mary] (Paris: Beauchesnes et Cie, 1908), 242 and 313. *Admirable Heart of Mary*, by St. John Eudes is available from Loreto Publications.

[221] Devotion to the Heart of Jesus has its foundation not in the revelations of Paray, which are private in nature, but rather in theology, in the Gospel, in Catholic Tradition. Nevertheless these revelations served to make this devotion easy, attractive and popular and to promote the spread of it. They lent it a concrete form, a special physiognomy, so that this devotion, as it is practiced today, proceeds completely and exclusively from St. Margaret Mary.

[222] St. Margaret Mary, I, 243.

[223] St. Margaret Mary, II, 428.

[224] [Archbishop] Pasquale Morganti, *Vos dixi amicos: il sacerdote e il Sacro Cuore* (Rome: Francesco Ferrari, 1920), introduction.

[225] Leo XIII, *Encyclical Mirae caritatis* (28 May 1902).

[226] According to the old philosophy and theology, which refer to the psychological concepts of that time, the heart was regarded as an organ of

express will of our Lord, honoring His Sacred Heart should have the character of Eucharistic atonement.

Holy Communions, hours of adoration, visits to the Most Blessed Sacrament, participation in Holy Mass: this is what our Lord first and emphatically asked of St. Margaret Mary, when He revealed to her—always in front of the tabernacle—the Gospel of His Heart. Here too, according to the writings of the saints, we find the most accessible and effective means of satisfying an ardent longing and inexhaustible thirst for the God of love.

This explains why the indifference of many priests toward the adorable Heart of the Redeemer logically goes hand in hand with their regrettable apathy toward the tabernacle. When you see them, you are almost tempted to doubt, not only their love, but even their faith. It is undeniable that people generally, even among the clergy, do not love the Heart of Jesus enough. And the main reason is no doubt that they do not think enough about the fact that it is a living heart, alive with the fullness of God's life.

It will not be difficult for you to admit that, due to the force of habit or a lack of active attention, you spend entire days near the Most Blessed Sacrament and yet are no more moved or thrilled than in the vicinity of a relic, however valuable or important it may be; after all, it is senseless and lifeless. And you know better than I the sad story of so many consecrated souls—*mysterium vobis dico*[227]—in whom the solemnity of the divine Sacrifice no longer produces a single thought about heaven, for whom the recollection and mysterious twilight of the sanctuary have become an intolerable burden. At the same time their visit with the divine Guest, which for a priest who is zealous for souls is a relief and an incomparable consolation, is the most boring moment of the day. They go to church as though they were going to their execution, and you might think that a repellent force drove them away from the holy temple again as soon as possible. Moreover their more or less pious posture, their repeated yawning and distraction reveals rather clearly that the Eucharistic Presence, which elicits strong feelings, undying excitement and divine inebriation from the saints, is for them only an interesting riddle.

---

love; according to most modern authors it should be regarded only as a *symbol* of love.

[227] "Behold, I tell you a mystery" (1Cor. 15:51)

The consequences of this way of acting are numerous and quite regrettable. The Angelic Doctor remarks that devotion *per se quidem et principaliter, spiritualem laetitiam mentis causat,*[228] and based on the same principle St. Augustine wrote *cantare amantis est.*[229] It follows that *the Sacrament of love* must also be *the Sacrament of joy: gaudium enim ex amore causatur.*[230] A soul cannot be contemplative unless it is Eucharistic, unless it intensely treasures God's gift *per quod spiritualis dulcedo suo fonte gustatur,*[231] "without enjoying interiorly the gift of God, without delighting in His presence and tasting the sweetness of the beloved Supreme Being that she possesses and adores".[232]

Do you remember the artless admission of St. Margaret Mary? "The Most Blessed Sacrament is the centerpiece of my heart, so that it finds no rest except in Its presence."[233]

---

[228] "Devotion produces of itself and principally spiritual joy" (St. Thomas Aquinas, *Summa Theologiae,* II-II, q. 82, art. 4, corp.).

[229] "Singing is a lover's thing" (St. Augustine, Sermo CCCXXXVI, 1; PL 33,1472). Cf. Désiré Félicien François Mercier, *La vie intérieure, appel aux âmes sacerdotales: retraite prêchée à ses prêtres* [The Interior Life, an appeal to priestly souls: a retreat preached to his priests] (Paris: Gabriel Beauchesne, 1922).

[230] "For joy is produced by love" (St. Thomas Aquinas, *Summa Theologiae,* II-II, q. 28, art. 1, corp.).

[231] "Through which spiritual sweetness is tasted at its source" (St. Thomas Aquinas, Opusculum 57 de Sacro Corpore Christi). He says in another passage: *Ex virtute hujus Sacramenti anima spiritualiter ... delectatur, et quodammodo inebriatur dulcedine bonitatis divinae* ["Through the power of this Sacrament the soul delights spiritually and is in a way inebriated by the sweetness of the divine goodness"] (*Summa Theologiae,* III, q. 79, art. 1, ad 2). *The Imitation of Christ* calls Jesus in the Most Blessed Sacrament *totius doctor consolationis internae* ["Thou impartest much consolation"], after remarking that *suavitas ... in hoc Sacramento, tanquam in fonte, plenarie latet* ["Thy sweetness ... plentifully lies hid in this Sacrament, as in its fountain"] (Thomas à Kempis, *The Imitation of Christ,* Book IV, Chapter 4).

[232] Dom Chautard, *Innerlichkeit,* Part III, Chapter 3. "Holy Communion is the beatitude of this life," wrote Father Louis Lallemant, S.J., *La doctrine spirituelle* (Paris: Desclée de Brouwer, 2011), princ. 6, sect. II, chap. 2, art. 5.

[233] St. Margaret Mary, II, 603. One day she said: "Jesus, I would like to

St. Francis de Sales lived in such intimate union with the Eucharistic Jesus that he could have answered someone who asked him the reason for his serious demeanor and his faithfulness to virtue: "I am preparing to celebrate Mass."[234]

A priest without deep, heartfelt piety, without any attraction to the Eucharist—*opus non minus miraculosum quam creatio rerum, vel etiam formatio corporis Christi in utero virginali*[235]—a priest without fine sympathy and affection for the Sacred Host (affection is the flower of love), is certainly an abnormal phenomenon in the world of souls, something like a star that has lost its natural center of gravity and now hurtles on a crazy course toward inevitable destruction.[236]

This is the reason—and the case is not uncommon—why the noblest of all ministries becomes a job like any other: *Nomen habes quod vivas, et mortuus es.*[237]

But let us investigate even more thoroughly this slow *apostasy of love*. Then we find the first traces in that stage of our life when we gave up prayer, which is the soul's breathing. So step by step we lost an understanding for supernatural things and treated the Most Blessed Sacrament as a mere *holy object*, no more, no less. It is one of our chief concerns to contemplate the Sacred Host

---

be consumed in longing for You." And Jesus replied: "Your longing has impressed My Heart so deeply that if I had not instituted this Sacrament of love, I would do so now so as to become your food" (II, 105, 364).

[234] André Jean Marie Hamon, *Vie de Saint François de Sales: Évêque et Prince de Genève* (Paris: Victor Lecoffre, 193043).

[235] "A no less miraculous work than the creation of all things, or even the formation of Christ's Body in the Virgin's womb" (St. Thomas Aquinas, *Summa theologiae*, III, q. 78, art. 4, arg. 2; Albertus Magnus, *In IV libros Sententiarum, distinctio* XXIV, a. 30).

[236] Often priests cite the need for social action as an excuse to conceal and justify their indifference toward the Most Blessed Sacrament. In contrast, St. Thomas Aquinas said clearly and distinctly that the ministry of a priest consists above all in fulfilling his conventional duties toward the true Body of Jesus and only *secondarily* in attending to the needs of the Mystical Body, *i.e.* of souls. Yet this second task *is not as essential* for the priesthood as the first (*In IV libros Sententiarum Magistri Petri Lombardi expositio, distinctio* XXIV, q. 1, art. 3: *sacerdos habet duos actus: unum principaliter supra corpus Christi verum; et alterum secundarium supra corpus Christi mysticum).*

[237] "Thou hast the name of being alive, and thou art dead" (Apoc. 3:1).

as *a person*? As a *living person*? And do we think enough about the fact—have we ever thought about it seriously?—that this is a *divine person*? *Ubi tu, ibi caelum*, says the author of *The Imitation of Christ* to our Lord.[238] It is certain that the slightest doubt in this regard—even more than an error against the faith—is a sin against charity.

Let us make sure that we understand each other. I am not asking whether you preach about the Real Presence; I am asking whether you are really convinced of it, interiorly and profoundly, *i.e.* whether you are ready, like the martyrs, to lay down your life for this truth, whether you are so convinced of it that you are able to subordinate *everything* that interests and concerns you to what interests and concerns Jesus in the Most Blessed Sacrament. I am asking whether your liturgical demeanor and your everyday life really are the expression of this firm, sincere and explicit faith: "In the Sacred Host, whose guardian I am, *the Word of God lives*, the Creator of the universe; and the most insignificant atom as well as the most dazzling of all suns obediently await the commands of His will!" Do you often sense an irresistible need to repeat enthusiastically before the sacred ciborium the words of St. Peter: *Tu es Christus, Filius Dei vivi?*[239]

This indifference, which basically is all too widespread, which the saints have so often lamented and condemned, this irreverent coldness toward the great mystery, the center of Christian life, this neglect that appears incomprehensible in a servant of God and becomes the scandal and the ruin of souls, has always had a disastrous effect on devotion to the Sacred Heart of Jesus.

In fact it is true—*scientibus legem loquor*[240]—that we would be obliged to adore this Sacred Heart, even on the sad hypothesis that It dwelt only in Paradise. But the moment faith opens up for us the path through the very gentle darkness of the tabernacle and reveals to us the whole splendor of a supernatural world, all the glories of divine life, in a place where the senses only perceive lifeless matter, there chiefly, in the Sacred Host, we should seek and adore this divine Heart which has so loved mankind.[241]

---

[238] "Where Thou art, there is heaven" (Thomas à Kempis, *The Imitation of Christ,* Book III, Chapter 59).
[239] "Thou art Christ, the Son of the living God" (Mt. 16:16).
[240] "I speak to them that know the law" (Rom. 7:1).
[241] It is superfluous to recall that the Sacred Heart of Jesus really deserves

A Eucharist that was without life for us, a ciborium that resembled a grave more than the dwelling place of a king, would inevitably make us think of an icy heart through which neither the pulsations of a God's Blood nor the almighty trembling of a God-man's soul coursed. It would still remain a sacred object, but it would surely be ill suited to awaken enthusiastic faith and heartfelt intimacy.

Defending us against this fatal reef, which threatens everyone who must constantly deal with holy things and with the most awe-inspiring of all mysteries, is devotion to the Eucharistic Heart of Jesus, in Whose honor the maternal care of Holy Mother Church recently instituted a special feast day.[242]

---

the absolute worship of *latria*, just like the entire human nature of the Redeemer, considered as a whole or in every one of its constituent parts, and that the honors shown to the Heart of Jesus ultimately belong to the whole person of the God-man. *Honor adorationis proprie debetur hypostasi subsistenti, tamen ratio honoris potest esse aliquid non subsistens, propter quod honoratur persona cui illus inest* ["Adoration is due to the subsisting hypostasis: yet the reason for honoring may be something non-subsistent, on account of which the person, in whom it is, is honored"] (St. Thomas Aquinas, *Summa Theologiae,* III, q. 25, art. 2, corp.). Nevertheless the Angelic Doctor remarked that we can adore the humanity of Jesus Christ (and consequently His Heart) not only with the *adoratione latriae, propter suam divinitatem* ["adoration of latria, on account of His divinity"], but also with the *adoratione duliae, propter perfectionem humanitatis* ["adoration of dulia on account of the perfection of His humanity"]. The Sacred Heart of Jesus, regarded as separate from the person of the Eternal Word, deserves only the relative cult of latria as *symbol of the Person of Christ,* to whom this Heart belongs (Terrien, *La dévotion au Sacré-Coeur,* 20; cf. Chapter 1, note 26 of this book).

[242] Cf. *Acta Apostolicae Sedis,* 13:545: *Pro feria V post octavam Ss. Corporis Christi, Sacratissimi Cordis Iesu Eucharistici officium proprium cum respondente missa approbatur* (9 November 1921). ["For the Thursday after the Octave of Corpus Christi, a proper office of the Most Sacred Eucharistic Heart of Jesus is approved, along with the corresponding Mass."] This is the latest confirmation of a cult that from Pius IX (1868) until now [1937] has been approved in 30 papal documents and in over 120 official episcopal documents. After various sad and also fortunate vicissitudes, this cult has found a place on the Church's liturgical calendar with its own Office

This devotion, which in its liturgical application is *new* yet, if you will, as *ancient* in its dogmatic foundations as Christianity itself, aims to indicate more clearly and fruitfully the attraction and ordering of souls to the mystery of love; "it is a divine gift proceeding from the very Heart of the Redeemer."[243] At the same time this devotion makes the worship of the Eucharist even more attractive and helps souls to enter more profoundly into the mystery of the Sacred Heart, this inexhaustible source that "causes the Eucharistic Blood to be poured forth over the world".[244]

Pater Sanctifica Eos[245]

Therefore let us not forget: If the Supreme Shepherd deemed it good to fasten even more closely the already existing ties between Eucharistic worship and devotion to the Sacred Heart of Jesus—ties that have developed naturally and traditionally—then at the same time he wanted to point out to the servants of God, who have such an urgent need for help, consolation and defense, where they can find the living Heart of the eternal High Priest, so as to show in It, *fons totius sacerdoti*,[246] the active, proximate principle, the chief motive as well as the ultimate reason for their *ascent to holiness*.

I intentionally say *ascent to holiness*, for "the love of my God is a merciless tyrant who never says: That is enough!"[247] I utilize therefore the expression *sanctity* and not the word *virtue*, because I am convinced that even if a priest leads a blameless and outwardly edifying life but wants nothing to do with becoming a *saint*, he robs God of a great honor, he loses a treasure of merits and thus weakens in an astonishing way the effectiveness

---

and Mass for the Thursday within the Octave of the Feast of the Sacred Heart. It is the victorious answer to all the objections and critiques that have been raised against it for a long time (see the works of Fathers Caste-lain, Garénaux, Krebs and Lejeune about the *Eucharistic Heart*).

[243] Leo XIII, *Encyclical Mirae caritatis* (28 May 1902).

[244] Terrien, *op. cit.,* 273.

[245] "Father, sanctify them" [Jn. 17:17].

[246] "Source of all priesthood" (St. Thomas Aquinas, *Summa Theologiae,* III, q. 20, art. 4, corp.).

[247] St. Margaret Mary, II, 523.

of his apostolate. *Sanctity,* therefore, is what the Lord expects of us. *In hoc clarificatus est pater meus,* UT FRUCTUM PLURIMUM AFFERATIS.[248] The relatively limited number of those who respond to this invitation should prompt us to be generous and not be an excuse or a pretext for our laziness.

You know this: there are plenty of mediocre priests; nor is there a lack of good ones, thank God. But all too rarely do we find in the Church *saintly* priests, apostles of the Heart of Jesus, who are willing to accept everything, to sacrifice everything, to suffer everything with faith and enthusiasm, to perform all their duties for love of Him and for His honor, without hesitating, without self-seeking calculations, without compromises, without petty restrictions, *spiritu ferventes,*[249] who are willing to be consumed completely and generously for Him like a burning candle... that is set on the lamp stand or even is forgotten under a bushel basket, as an apostle or as a victim of His love: *considerantes idcirco se quotidie calicem sanguinis Christi bibere, ut possint et ipsi propter Christum sanguinem fundere.*[250]

And yet sanctity is for those who serve at the altar a *duty of their state in life*[251] and at the same time a right of Christian souls. Whoever wants to be an administrator of the mysteries of God[252] must also for this reason strive to become *sanctus, innocens, impollutus, segregatus a peccatoribus,*[253] according to St. Paul's admonition, *ut filii lucis*

---

[248] "In this is my Father glorified: that you bring forth very much fruit" (Jn. 15:8).

[249] "In spirit fervent" (Rom. 12:11).

[250] "Who consider that they drink each day from the chalice of Christ's Blood, so that they themselves too might be able to shed their blood for Christ" (St. Cyprian of Carthage, *Epistola LVI ad Thibaritanos de exhortatione martyrii,* PL 4, 350).

[251] Clerics should cultivate the interior, spiritual life more than laymen and outwardly behave themselves accordingly as well, so that in their thoughts and in their conduct they might be examples to the laity (cf. Codex Iuris Canonici, 1917, canon 124: *Clerici debent sanctiorem prae laicis vitam interiorem et exteriorem ducere eisque virtute et recte factis in exemplum excellere*; St. Thomas Aquinas, Summa theologiae, II-II, q. 184, art. 8, corp.).

[252] 1Cor. 4:1.

[253] "Holy, innocent, undefiled, separated from sinners" (Heb. 7:26).

ambulate; fructus enim lucis est in omni bonitate et justitia.[254]

For this reason, the spotless glory of our life must be a constant striving for all that uplifts and improves, a perpetual rejection of whatever is demeaning and a merciless condemnation of anything that defiles. Our name should be a symbol of the triumph of the most magnanimous ideals, a sign of contradiction to all debasement and all slavery. It goes without saying, and this is certainly an argument that should not be neglected: If we grow in perfection, then we contribute far more and far better by that alone to the salvation of souls than by any outward action. *Pro eis sanctifico meipsum, ut sint et ipsi sanctificati in veritate.*[255]

Before I conclude this short presentation of the relations between the Sacred Heart of Jesus and the Most Blessed Sacrament of the altar, I must draw the reader's attention to one other very important point. Have you ever reflected seriously on this intimate, gentle bond that unites the priesthood with the Holy Eucharist? If the tabernacle is the mysterious center around which priestly vocations especially flourish and develop, *vinum germinans virgines,*[256] on the other hand the Real Presence of Jesus in the Sacrament of His love no doubt depends *solely and necessarily* on our exalted ministry as consecrators. And just as the express agreement and the free, active cooperation of Mary was necessary in order for the Eternal Word to take on this Body and this human Heart, which are constantly present under the consecrated species,[257] so too He wishes to use us alone as His instruments in order to accomplish the Sacrifice of the altar.[258]

---

[254] "Walk then as children of the light. For the fruit of the light is in all goodness and justice" (Eph. 5:8-9).

[255] "For them do I sanctify myself, that they also may be sanctified in truth" (Jn. 17:19).

[256] "Wine springing forth virgins" (Zach. 9:17).

[257] In this sense Gerson calls the Most Blessed Virgin Mary "the Mother of the Eucharist". An old preface from the time of St. Gregory the Great prayed as follows to the Mother of God: *Lacta, Mater, cibum nostrum* ["Nourish with your milk, O Mother, our Food"]. In connection with the Procession with the Blessed Sacrament, Dom Guéranger reminds us that in a medieval church the Sacred Host destined for the Corpus Christi Procession was placed in the hands of a Marian statue, which served as a monstrance. Here too art is at the service of the liturgy, so as to express a theological idea tenderly.

[258] The priest speaks *nomine Christi et potestate ordinis* ["in Christ's name

What a consoling thought, capable of sustaining in a soul the ecstasy of love and gratitude, which grow into an infinite esteem for our vocation and trust in the inexhaustible fruitfulness of our ministry. In order to redeem mankind in the first place and also for the daily application of the abundant fruits of His "plenteous redemption" to souls of good will, the Lord took His kindness so far that He placed His omnipotence into the hands of a creature and made it the direct, necessary instrument of His merciful designs.[259]

If Jesus in fact decided to keep the glorious wounds of His bloody Passion in His glorified Body, and in His adorable Heart the interior disposition of a soul that is both priest and victim—*Sacerdos in aeternum..., Agnus tanquam occisus*[260]—if He willed to reveal His feelings just once in the tragedy of His sufferings, *introivit semel in sancta*,[261] then His love has assigned to us the very tender task of representing every day the perceptible, unbloody expression of His interior, lasting decrees, which He has never revoked. He wills to make the souls that He has redeemed dependent on the celebration of the divine mysteries— an exclusively, preeminently priestly action, which each of us performs 18,000 times in fifty years of this ministry—the daily, ceaseless outpouring of the merits of His Blood upon them, the Blood of His Heart. Since the Eucharistic Presence is essentially connected with the sacrifice of the altar, through which alone the "miracle of love" is perpetuated down through the centuries, it is certain that we owe solely to the free, effective collaboration of the priest the fact that this very same Heart that lives and reigns in the glory of the Father also lives and reigns in the humiliations of His sacramental state.[262]

---

and by the power of Holy Orders"] the words of the rite with which is bound up *vis creata effectiva consecrationis* ["the created power to effect the consecration"] (St. Thomas Aquinas, *Summa Theologiae*, III, q. 78, art. 4, corp. and arg. 1).

[259] Here we are considering the fact in retrospect, according to the present order of Divine Providence.

260 "A priest for ever" (Ps. 109/110:4)... "a Lamb as it were slain" (Apoc. 5:6).

[261] "Christ... entered once [for all] into the [Holy of] Holies" (Heb. 9:12).

[262] These are the conclusions drawn by Father Giuseppe M. Petazzi, S.J., in his excellent booklet *La vera natura del s. Sacrificio dell'altare: studio*

The Demands of Love

To us too, the official honor guard of the tabernacle, the outpost of the Sacred Heart of Jesus, everything should speak about the close relations that exist between these two devotions. Whatever the cost, we must in a special way create an atmosphere of personal and real holiness around the Sacred Host. Besides, the best of all occupations for a loving heart is to take pains.

Therefore let unclean hands and those that perform work for hire stay away from the lamp that flickers near the tabernacle; let us tend to it ourselves; let it be clean and lit at all times; let it say something to Him about us and to us about Him. After all, it is like the lighthouse that directs souls that are driven about by the world's storms to the haven of salvation in the Heart of Jesus, "the light of the world".

On the altar, close by the tabernacle, let there always be beautiful, fragrant fresh flowers—real flowers—and if possible those that we ourselves have raised, picked and arranged, or that have been picked and arranged at our bidding. They are broken, sacrificed lives in the service of the King of Love, in order to pay honor to the Heart of the Almighty and to sing the praises of Him who deigned to be called "the flower of Jesse's stem" and the "lily of the valleys".

The altar linens, the altar cloths and corporals should always be clean, neatly ironed and, if possible, artistically or at least tastefully designed. They form the royal garments of this incarnate Word,

---

teologico-filosofico [The True Nature of the Holy Sacrifice of the Altar: theological-philosophical essay] (Rome: Messaggero del Sacro Cuore, 1925). The pious and learned author summarizes in 36 pages everything that the best authors have written about this obscure, difficult question and sheds light on the most debated points. According to him, Holy Mass alone is the physical, unbloody expression of Jesus' interior sacrifice, which was expressed in a bloody manner on the Cross. He points out that His interior dispositions as priest and victim are the true element of the Sacrifice of Calvary and that they continue to exist in the soul of the risen Jesus. When we consecrate the bread and the wine separately, we express outwardly the interior sacrifice of the glorified Redeemer. Therefore the priest performs an action without which the renewal of the Sacrifice of Calvary would be impossible; in other words: We supply the necessary material for the reality of the Sacrifice of the Altar (p. 24).

which has set up Its throne in heaven to be the bliss of the angels and saints, and of Him who remains on the altars on earth in order to gladden mankind.[263]

But what should I say first about the person of God's servant, the servant of the Sacred Heart of Jesus, *vicarius amoris Christi* [representative of Christ's love]?

To Holy Church, twelve years in seminary do not seem too long to instill into our hearts the virtues of the eternal High Priest, to strengthen them against the seductions of the flesh, to examine with zealous diligence and motherly care whether our eyes and lips are clean enough, whether are hands are not too unworthy, to touch the adorable Heart of the Son of God directly and frequently with an impressive familiarity and to distribute His immaculate Flesh to the faithful. If he comes daily into contact with the divine in this way, then how much the priest's soul and body should be sanctified day by day. *Estote ergo imitatores Dei, sicut filii charissimi, et ambulate in dilectione!*[264]

Read from time to time the sacred expressions [of the rite of ordination] in the Roman Pontifical. They were addressed to you, to each one of you personally, at an extremely solemn moment—do you still remember it?

Amodo vigiles, ... amodo sobrii, ... amodo casti, in vera et catholica fide fundati, ... estote nitidi, mundi, puri, ... sicut decet ministros Christi.[265] How easy all these sacrifices, renunciation and separation seemed to us then.... Was it not for the Sacred Heart of Jesus? *Ubi autem amor, labor non est, sed sapor.*[266]

And the bishop continued, pointing out to us the guidelines of priestly perfection: *ut cunctis ... caelestis vitae formam praebeant, ... ut Sanctae Ecclesiae exemplo sanctitatis consulant, ... ut se, et alios, et Dei Ecclesiam illuminent; ... abundet in eis totius forma virtutis,*

---

[263] With his usual gift of penetrating insight, St. Augustine shows how the Word of God is the food of angels and of men.

[264] "Be ye therefore followers of God, as most dear children: and walk in love" (Eph. 5:1-2).

[265] "From now on be vigilant; in the future be sober, from now on be chaste, firmly founded on the true Catholic faith.... Be refined, clean, pure.... as befits servants of Christ."

[266] "Where there is love, there is no toil, but rather relish" (St. Bernard of Clairvaux, *Tractatus de caritate, inter opusculos,* PL 84, 59).

pudor constans, innocentiae puritas, ... caelestis sapientia, probi mores, diuturna justitiae observatio; ... ceterasque virtutes in se ostendant, exemplo praebeant, admonitione confirment, ... ut gravitate actuum, et censura vivendi, probent se seniores.[267]

This was the burnt offering of "the old man" [cf. Eph 4:22-24] on the altar of Christ's love, the necessary and very sweet sacrifice of ourselves. For we knew very well that this ideal demands worship and that the worship most pleasing to God is the sacrifice of ourselves. And yet that was only the *first step* on our glorious *via crucis* [Way of the Cross].

In fact it is not enough to have accepted this with full awareness, to have promised this with admirable generosity. It is necessary to satisfy the longing of the Sacred Heart of Jesus faithfully and zealously. And this Heart abhors all sacrilegious theft, *rapinam in holocausto*.[268]

How much material there is here for serious reflection and examination, at the feet of Jesus in the Most Blessed Sacrament! At His feet, because He alone can give us light and strength, He *in quo est tota sacerdotii plenitudo*,[269] He, the "holy teacher who teaches sanctity".[270] If we should feel weak, if we, after having offered up the Sacred Host [in Latin *Hostia*, Victim] so many times, had yet to sacrifice entirely the "human victim", i.e. our sinful body; if after all these promises we still had to lament so many falls into sin, then we should take refuge with the saintly Cyrene, so as to commend ourselves to Him who can save us. *Cum enim infirmor, tunc potens*

---

[267] "That they may show to all a heavenly way of life, ... that they may give to Holy Church an example of holiness, ... that they may enlighten themselves and others and the Church of God, ... that they may abound in every sort of virtue, constant purity, spotless innocence, ... heavenly wisdom, proven morals and the constant practice of justice, ... may they model other virtues, teach by their example, confirm by their admonition, ... so that through the seriousness of their conduct and their disciplined way of life they may prove themselves as elders" (*Pontificale Romanum, De Ordinibus Sacris*).

[268] "Robbery in a holocaust" (Isa. 61:8).

[269] "In whom is the fullness of the priesthood" (St. Thomas Aquinas, *Summa Theologiae*, III, q. 63, art. 6, corp.).

[270] St. Margaret Mary, II, 67.

sum; ... non ego autem, sed gratia Dei mecum.[271] Along the steep path of our personal sanctification, as well as in the difficult enterprise of leading souls to the Sacred Heart of Jesus, we need a living, active faith in His Eucharistic Presence, and we ourselves must give an example, so that the crowd that for a long time has had nothing to eat *oculis, magis quam auribus credant.*[272]

If the Eucharistic Presence, the proximity of the tabernacle is already an effective means of moral perfection, what can we say then about the guarantees of sanctity offered to us by Holy Mass and consequently by our daily union in Holy Communion with this adorable Heart of the Redeemer? If it is an indescribable advantage to live close to Him, what advantage will it be to be nourished by Him? True God and perfect man, is He not the efficient cause, the instrument, the meritorious and exemplary cause of all holiness?[273]

Happy the soul of the priest for whom the most intimate union with the Heart of Jesus becomes *medicina omnis spiritualis languoris,*[274] a loving, everyday necessity, so to speak! Blessed that mingling that reminds us so closely of the miracle of the Hypostatic Union! An exalted convergence between the divine and the human, which will be surpassed in intensity only by the splendor of the beatific vision! *O quam magnum suscipit Dominum! Quam dilectum inducit hospitem! Quam jucundum recipit socium! Quam fidelem acceptat amicum!*[275]

---

[271] "For when I am weak, then am I powerful" (2Cor. 12:10); "Yet not I, but the grace of God with me" (1Cor. 15:10).

[272] "That they might believe more through their eyes than through their ears" (Letter of St. Francis de Sales to Monseigneur Frémyot, Archbishop of Bourges).

[273] St. Thomas Aquinas, *Summa Theologiae*, III, q. 48, art. 6 and q. 49, art. 1.

[274] A medicine for all spiritual infirmity (cf. Thomas à Kempis, *The Imitation of Christ*, Book IV, Chapter 3).

[275] "Oh, how great a Lord does [the soul] entertain! How beloved a guest does she bring into her house! How sweet a companion does she receive! How faithful a friend does she welcome!" (Thomas à Kempis, *The Imitation of Christ*, Book IV, Chapter 3).

The elect possess God through the beatific vision, whereas we possess Him through faith alone. But sacramental Communion, like the beatific vision, gives Him to us immediately, completely, without further intermediary and without any other obstacles than our sins and our tepidity alone.

In the midst of our daily struggles, dangers and snares, while facing tireless, stiff-necked foes, we want to be nourished in faith with the Flesh of the Lamb who is also the Lion of Juda.... His adorable Body is our wartime rations, *annona praeliantium, cibus grandium*;[276] His Blood cleanses us from all sin[277] and is for us the pledge of eternal life. *Qui manducat me, et ipse vivet propter me*.[278]

The world, in which the disastrous work of the sects weakens the faith and tries to extinguish it, surrounds us with its noise and pleasures; in its relentless, terrible and perverse logic it becomes drunk on the cup of pleasure and plunges laughing into every bog.... A demonic conspiracy works to make us fall too or at least to cover us with dirt. And yet Jesus wants us to be holy, "as also your heavenly Father is".[279]

Only have courage! *Sursum corda!* [Lift up your hearts!] He is "the God of hope, peace and love".[280] Why should we fear? *Tantummodo crede..., omnia possibilia sunt credenti*.[281] Yesterday you received the Most Sacred Heart of Jesus, today It will once again become your food, if you wish; tomorrow, have no doubt, It will join with you again.... Only a matter of twenty-four hours! Be strong, fight valiantly; *nondum enim usque ad sanguinem restitistis*.[282] Think about it: only a few hours, and then once again you will climb the steps of the altar to this God, "who gives joy to your

---

If our faith were sufficiently lively to remove this tepidity and to expand our heart, our love would be ardent enough to overcome every obstacle and to prepare ourselves to receive the Sacred Host, just as the purifying punishments of Purgatory prepare the soul for the beatific vision; then the effects would be about the same, and Christians satisfied by the Eucharistic life would be already on this earth transformed by means of Holy Communion into God, as the elect are by means of glory.

[276] "The rations of those who do battle, the food of the great" (St. Augustine, *Enarrationes in Psalmos CXLIII: Sermo ad plebem,* 10; PL 37, 1863).

[277] 1Jn. 1:7.

[278] "He that eateth me, the same also shall live by me" (Jn. 6:58).

[279] Mt. 5:48

[280] Cf Rom. 15:13 and 2Cor. 13:11.

[281] "Only believe, ... all things are possible to him that believeth" (Mk. 5:36; 9:22).

[282] "For you have not yet resisted unto blood" (Heb. 12:4).

youth".[283] His Blood will purple your lips, His grace will surround you as a shield; a new "bath of love"[284] awaits you. *Beati oculi qui vident quae vos videtis.*[285]

What unexplored horizons are opened up to the eyes of our faith by devotion to the Heart of Jesus, who lives in the Sacred Host! And how salutary and beneficial this faith in His love will be for us! This most gentle Heart becomes once again for us the key to all mysteries, the explanation of all dogmas, the solution to all problems. This Heart alone is enough to accept into Itself all the exuberance of our youthful activity, to instill in us a new enthusiasm for our ministry, to give new growth to our piety, to make us use our God-given talents in practice, and to raise us to a high degree of sanctity and of sanctifying others.

The Long Study and the Great Love

As servants of the sanctuary, let us enliven our faith, shake off this unwarranted rigidity and this gloomy mistrust which all too often cripple our spiritual powers and even endanger the fruits of our apostolate: *surge qui dormis..., et illuminabit te Christus.*[286] Let us anoint our whole life with devotion to the Heart of Jesus, *bonitate et amore plenum.*[287] Let us take Him, and Him alone, as the principle, means, and goal of our activity, so as to be able to renew the world in love. Let Him be our wealth, our strength, our joy, our peace, our consolation, our hope, our salvation, our life; *et quis tam vita cordium, quam Deus meus Jesus?*[288]

"He has a burning desire to be known, loved and honored by men.[289] His Most Sacred Heart contains incomprehensible

---

[283] Cf. Ps 42:4.

[284] This expression comes from the saintly Curé of Ars.

[285] "Blessed are the eyes that see the things which you see" (Lk. 10:23).

[286] "Rise, thou that sleepest, and arise from the dead: and Christ shall enlighten thee" (Eph. 5:14).

[287] "Full of kindness and love" (Litany of the Sacred Heart).

[288] "But who could be the life of hearts as much as Thou, Jesus, my God?" (St. Bernard of Clairvaux, *Tractatus de caritate, inter opusculos,* PL 184, 599).

[289] St. Margaret Mary, II, 530.

treasures, which He wants to pour out into all hearts of good will; this is indeed one last endeavor of His love for sinners."[290]

I cannot remain silent about the fact that this cult, which is priestly to the highest degree and can be described as the epitome of Christianity, the summary of the whole religion, is connected with too many dogmas for anyone from our ranks to be able to disregard a diligent, persistent, in-depth and complete investigation of the principles that justify it. If we want to silence its numerous enemies—old offshoots of Jansenism and more and more new buds of Modernism—we must be very exact in our terminology and have clear, precise ideas in mind. Woe to those who are unable to avoid vague, confused language, *docentes ea quae non oportet.*[291]

To the utmost sorrow of my soul, I have met priests who were unfamiliar with the most elementary concepts of the theology of the Sacred Heart of Jesus; when they opened their mouths they were necessarily "blind and leaders of the blind".[292] Anyone in such a lamentable condition of culpable spiritual poverty is consequently, among other things, in violation of the directives of canon law,[293] and so the best service that he can perform for this devotion in this case (and only in this one) is to maintain a reverent silence. On the other hand, though, it is our sacred duty, before reaching such a low point, to provide ourselves with the necessary education, especially since the grace of priesthood makes it easy for us to acquire what St. Paul calls *eminentem scientiam Jesu Christi.*[294]

Consequently we should feel compelled to investigate in particular the theological foundations of this devotion; let us research its origin, follow its historical development, consider the attention paid to it by the Roman popes and the bishops. Let us meditate on its meaning, its necessity, its beauty, its harmony, and its similarities to other forms of worship, its splendid fruitfulness, its vigorous spread. Let us examine more closely the consequences for

---

[290] St. Margaret Mary, II, 530.

[291] "Teaching things which they ought not" (Tit. 1:11).

[292] Mt. 15:14.

[293] "Clerics should continue their studies, especially of theology, even after receiving priestly orders" (*Codex Iuris Canonici, 1917, can. 129: Clerici studia, praesertim sacra, recepto sacerdotio, ne intermittant*).

[294] "The excellent knowledge of Jesus Christ" (Phil. 3:8).

individuals and its advantages for society in its liturgical applications and in its artistic depictions. Let us appreciate its pedagogical and pastoral value; let us strive to become as thoroughly acquainted as possible with the ascetical, apologetic, hagiographic and polemical literature about this devotion, the canonical decisions that concern the object, goal, the various elements and the practical means thereof: and in light of the high praises of it sung by the saints, we will acknowledge with heartfelt joy the resplendent crown of glory that makes it appear so miraculous and dear to souls.

Study alone is not enough, however, when it is a question of grasping and assimilating a spiritual doctrine. Above all it is by good contemplative prayer—with attention, devotion, humility and zeal—that one can taste in full measure the marvels hidden in this form of Catholic piety: *Qui didicerunt a Christo mites esse et humiles corde, plus cogitando et orando proficiunt, quam legendo et audiendo.*[295] In the meek ejaculations, the beneficial outpourings, and the infinitely active recollection of private prayer, in the majestic, solemn rites of Holy Mass, in the Divine Office that radiates with beauty ever new, in the serious, impressive teachings of the liturgy we must seek the Sacred Heart of Jesus. *Disce Cor Dei in verbis Dei, ut ardentius ad aeterna suspires.*[296]

---

[295] "Those who have learned from Christ to be meek and lowly of heart (Mt 11:29) learned it better through meditation and prayer than through reading and listening [to preaching]" (St. Augustine, *Epistola CXLVII ad Paulinam: Docet Deum corporeis oculis videri non posse,* 1; PL 33, 597).

St. Thomas Aquinas remarked on this subject: *Contemplatio spiritualis pulchritudinis vel bonitatis est principium amoris spiritualis* ["Spiritual contemplation of beauty or good is the beginning of spiritual love"] (Summa theologiae, I-II, q. 27, art. 2, corp.).

296 "Learn the Heart of God in the words of God, so that you might ardently long for eternal things" (St. Gregory the Great, *Registri epistolarum, liber IV, epistola XXXI;* PL 77, 706).

St. Augustine calls Sacred Scripture too "the Heart of Christ". How desirable it would be, if seminary instruction and theology faculties made more room for the Sacred Heart of Jesus! Would we then have to oblige priests who have completed their studies in theology to become students again, if they want to learn clear, well-founded concepts about such an important and practical question as this? Why not present this devotional practice to our young Levites at the beginning of their ecclesiastical curriculum, which is riddled with visible and hidden thorns, when they still

Moreover one should not indulge in any illusions: To know the Heart of Jesus is good; to love It is better, *quia amor ipse notitia est*,[297] and it would be useless to want to study It unless we had resolved to assimilate in our life the consequences that follow from these theological principles. Devotion to the Sacred Heart of Jesus *demands intellectual reforms*; it also demands much more, however, a profound moral transformation. Through this devotion the love that matures the soul must become ready and willing, easy, serviceable and active... *probatio enim dilectionis, exhibitio est operis*.[298]

To revere this Heart that is so gentle means to know It and to make It known, by promoting Its cult, by proclaiming Its glory, by spreading Its dominion in society with an unshakable faith, by loving in the Heart of Jesus the infinite love that the Eucharist has given to the world, and by studying beneath the tabernacle the exuberance and delicacy of this divine love that the Sacred Heart has revealed to mankind.

That is not yet all. It goes without saying: This devotion should not be imposed by force. Even if it is accepted with docility as a hard necessity of our times, it will never produce all its fruits. In order to become an effective instrument of sanctification and salvation, it must be practiced with true enthusiasm; it must become a *living* devotion. Just as it is not enough to love the Heart of Jesus in any old way and one must rather love It in a manner worthy of It, so too it is indispensable to lead a life of familiarity with It—to share one's everyday routine with It— to join with It in a sweet intimacy that is quite childlike and spontaneous, to take no step without asking It, to set ourselves aside sincerely, our talents, our merits, our toils and our desires, so that He alone may be glorified always and everywhere, at any cost: *Illum oportet crescere, me autem minui*.[299]

---

have the zeal of their initial enthusiasm? The Sacred Heart of Jesus would make their sacrifices less painful, the first dispelling of their illusions less bitter, their crosses less burdensome and their ascent to their Mount Calvary less rough.

[297] "For love itself is a kind of knowledge" (St. Gregory the Great, *Homilia XXVII in Evangelia: Habita ad populum in basilica sancti Pancratii martyris, die natalis ejus* [Jn. 15:12-16], II, 4; PL 76, 1207).

[298] "For the proof of love is the performance of work" (St. Gregory the Great, PL 76, 1220).

[299] "He must increase, but I must decrease" (Jn. 3:30).

"Love is the frequently repeated thought, the constant remembrance, it is the shared joys, sorrows and interests of life; it is dedication without calculation, it is the ardent need for presence and fellowship in all things, a union that is never satisfied and that always strives to grow until it has become true unity."[300] Hence it is indispensable to study the Redeemer's virtues, those of His human and those of His Eucharistic life, to grasp their value, their extent, their perfection, their importance, to love them and to practice them for the love of Him and for the sake of His glory, *religionis summa sit imitari quem colis*.[301] Through the words that have come forth from His divine mouth, we must maintain this profound reverence that causes us to worship the smallest particle of the consecrated Host with our forehead bent down to the dust of the earth, without hesitating or disputing.[302]

Fortis ut Mors Dilectio[303]

Loving the Heart of Jesus means being able to suffer much, always, alone, in silence, with a smile on one's lips, beneath that glance that searches hearts, completely forgetting the persons dear to us, without being understood, without finding sympathy or consolation; it means to hide the *sacred mystery of the cross*[304] as a priceless treasure in the ground of the pierced, dejected soul, in the middle of a heart crowned with thorns. Loving It means forgetting ourselves and our misery too, so as to think of Him alone who is the resurrection and the life, casting all our anxious cares about spiritual progress into this adorable Heart. And even if we fell a hundred times into the same imperfections, we would

---

[300] Mgr. Charles Louis Gay, *Sermons de l'Avent* [Advent Sermons] (Poitiers: H. Oudin, 1895, 1914; Paris: Alfred Mame et Fils: 19212), 335.

[301] "The epitome of religion is to imitate the one whom you revere" (St. Augustine, *De Civitate Dei*, Part I, Book 8, Chapter 17; PL 41, 242).

[302] Jesus revealed to St. Gertrude that the most precious of His relics are His words, as the Gospels report them to us (*Legatus divinae pietatis*, The Messenger of Divine Love, Book IV, Chapter 50).

[303] "Love is strong as death" (Cant. 8:6).

[304] From the hymn *Vexilla Regis* (Vespers from Palm Sunday to Wednesday of Holy Week, the Feast of the Exaltation of the Cross, Holy Thursday [reposition of the Blessed Sacrament of the Altar], Good Friday [Adoration of the Cross]).

always have to get up again immediately, humbly and calmly, while entrusting ourselves to the perpetual miracle of His all-powerful grace and to find our peace of mind again in the infinite sweetness of God's forgiveness.

Loving the Sacred Heart of Jesus means honoring the glorified wounds of the Crucified Lord in those who suffer and enfolding with gentle affection the pale, tortured members in whom He is pleased to renew each day the ineffable poem of His Passion and to continue it down the centuries forever.

Loving Him means having compassion with His sufferings and making reparation to Him, in will and in work, practically, effectively, tirelessly, generously and prudently, for the monstrous crimes by which His enemies defile His person, trample His honor, drag His dignity through the mire and insult His representatives. At the same time it means making reparation for the sins of all those who by their vocation and their free choice are supposed to be His friends—sins which considered objectively may perhaps be less serious but in reality are all the more offensive—but instead are *crucifying Him again.*[305]

Loving the Heart of Jesus means *in simplicitate cordis et sinceritate Dei*[306] being close to and helping everyone who spends himself for His glory, without regret, for the sake of the common good, renouncing so-called privileges or prerogatives based on a completed *diploma*..., and instead spreading the mantle of Christian charity over weakness and misery by silently forgiving and forgetting bitter words and crude behavior and thus carefully avoiding the injured honor, petty jealousies and ministerial envy that so often call into question the dignity and success of a just cause.

Loving means fulfilling faithfully and carefully one's modest duty in keeping with a monotonous, hidden life, without looking for praise or recognition, without putting down someone who is climbing, without restricting the endeavors of another person through an ill-concealed jealousy..., without rejoicing over his failure, without kicking a man who is down; without disregarding his service or suspecting his intentions—in a word, without hindering or condemning good for the sole reason that it does not come from our own workshop..., *dum omni modo ... Christus annuntietur.*[307]

---

[305] *Rursum crucifigentes* (Heb. 6:6).

[306] "In simplicity of heart and sincerity of God" (2Cor. 1:12).

[307] "So that by all means ... Christ [may] be preached" (Phil. 1:18).

Loving the Heart of Jesus means being content with necessary material things and joyfully contributing anything left over to the worship of God, to works of Catholic charity, to the seminaries, to poor convents, to the foreign missions, to whoever is hungry, suffering or needy, ill or "suffering persecution for justice' sake".[308] Loving means turning the gold, silver and pearls from our strongbox into works of radiant love of neighbor which no rust consumes and no thief diminishes; ... seeing to it that "stones turn to bread"[309] and that the unearned gifts of Divine Providence are transformed into instruments of mercy.

Loving the Sacred Heart means "giving It all the love that It expects from us: a strong love that does not let itself be oppressed; a pure love without admixture or selfishness; a crucified love that finds its joy only in suffering..., a preferential love of self-denial and renunciation, so as to allow the Beloved to act and to cut, burn and destroy in us anything that displeases Him."[310] That is why it is so necessary to allow Him to lead us and to work in us and around us, at every hour of the day and each day of the year, all the years of our life, to allow ourselves to be inebriated by the folly of the cross and to make the most difficult sacrifices, not only with fidelity and perfect submission to His intentions, but increasingly with an exuberant joy, *hilarem enim datorem diligit Deus;*[311] it means gratefully kissing the hand that strikes us and always blessing it, whether it gives gifts or takes them away.

Loving the heart of Jesus means passionately loving Holy Church, that virginal flower that sprang up from His Blood, and decisively rejecting every form and any appearance of literary, moral, dogmatic, canonical, historical or political modernism; gathering around this Church which is "the favorite of the Divine Heart",[312] in an ever more perfect union with her teaching, with an ever more complete submission to her precepts, whereby each of us becomes *obediens usque ad mortem.*[313] Loving means sharing

---

[308] Cf. Mt. 5:10.

[309] Cf. Mt. 4:3.

[310] St. Margaret Mary, II, 403.

[311] "God loveth a cheerful giver" (2Cor. 9:7).

[312] Cf. Eph. 5:25: "as Christ also loved the church and delivered himself up for it".

[313] "Obedient unto death" (Phil. 2:8).

with heartfelt sympathy in the triumphs and humiliations of the Supreme Shepherd, following the *sweet Christ on earth*[314] in all things and always, with erudition and promptness, obeying His commands, suggestions, recommendations and His express wishes, whatever form they may take or whoever the intermediary may be through whom they reach us; accepting them fully, even if they happen to contradict our personal opinions, our shortsighted view, the incessant demands of our self-interest, or the foolish sophistries with which injured self-love so wastefully associates.

Being subject to the Heart of Jesus with sincere devotion means burning with the desire to make It known and loved, extend Its reign, glorify Its name and carry out Its will, in whatever regard it may be revealed. This means loving the souls that have tasted Its Blood, loving them all, loving them with purity and sincerity, in the constant, perpetual and perfect renunciation of our own tastes, ideals and well-being.

How often perhaps we have thought that we were demeaning ourselves when we personally went to the trouble to instill a bit of piety in this rude, dirty, uneducated child; or to listen patiently and willingly to the ever-recurring complaints of poverty, or to set back on his feet and restore to decency a man who has fallen into the pit of disgrace! ...

Oh, how different was the price of grace for the enlightened outlook of the saints! "One soul", St. Charles Borromeo used to say, "is diocese enough for a bishop."[315] Who could forget the admonition of Cardinal Federico Borromeo to his clergy during the plague in Milan: "Welcome the plague with love, as if it were life, a reward, as soon as it means winning a soul for Christ."[316] "To cross the ocean, save a soul and die!" sighed Father Chicard, the apostle of China.[317]

---

[314] St. Catharine of Siena used this name for Him in her writings, just as she called the Church the sweet *Bride of Christ*.

[315] Cited from Henry Edward Cardinal Manning, *The Eternal Priesthood* (London, Burns and Oates, 1884), 83.

[316] Giuseppe Ripamonti, *De peste Mediolani quae fuit anno* 1630, vol. 5.

317 This remark was erroneously attributed to Fr. Chanel in an earlier Italian edition. Rev. Jean-Emmanuel Drochon, *Un Chevalier apôtre, Célestin-Godefroy Chicard, missionnaire de Yun-Nan* reported the remark, written down by Fr. Chicard in his own hand; consequently no doubt about it remains.

Certainly, a man who does not understand the infinite poetry of the saints' yearning as though through a divine inspiration is not worthy of the name and office of a priest. And even if he were to be snatched up to the third heaven, one might doubt the spirit that animates him, for the best and safest rapture—the one that crowns, confirms and consecrates God's gifts—is the "rapture of life and good works".[318]

Therefore if we truly want to be subject to the Heart of Him "who went about doing good",[319] we should offer up each day a little more of the human things that drag us down and allow ourselves to be governed more and more by the divine things that uplift and ennoble us. Let us reject more each day the flattering tyranny of pleasure so as to conform our life to the stern poetry of duty.

Certainly it seems very strange to you that a devotion that is supposed to combat selfishness and sensuality actively, so as to transform and deify man, still has stubborn opponents after all, even among those who are really not bad. These individuals just cannot understand what I said before: *Visa sunt ante illos sicut deliramentum verba ista.*[320] It may be that they too really want to love, but without causing themselves trouble, without suffering, without doing something for Jesus and for souls. They would gladly become saints, but in their own way, by hiding behind the paltry reasoning of a foolish individualism which is the product of a world of comfortable feelings, which is not the most serious but still the most widespread intellectual sickness of our era....

They do not know about the secret workings of the interior life, about the divine efficacy of prayer, the incomparable fruitfulness

---

[318] St. Francis de Sales, *Oeuvres de Saint François de Sales, Évêque et Prince de Genève et Docteur de l'Église* (Annecy: J. Niérat, 1892), 5:21 and 27.

St. Thomas Aquinas made the following remark: God is the true motive for our love of neighbor; consequently the act of love that has God as its object is identical in kind with the act of love that pertains to our neighbor (*Summa Theologiae*, II-II, q. 25, art. 1 and 2). Is this not commentary on the verse from St. John: *Qui enim non diligit fratrem suum quem videt, Deum, quem non videt, quomodo potest diligere?* ("For he that loveth not his brother whom he seeth, how can he love God whom he seeth not?") (1Jn. 4:20).

[319] Acts 10:38.

[320] "These words seemed to them as idle tales" (Lk. 24:11).

of sacrifice, the gentle sweetness of suffering, the inner peace of a holy life, the constant joy of an ineffable hope..., and yet these very things are the real, ordinary fruits of love for Jesus. Such men do not know that the holy flames of the apostolate belong to the nature of well-ordered love itself: *Numquam est Dei amor otiosus: operatur enim magna, si est; si vero operari renuit amor non est.*[321]

Centuplum Accipies[322]

What a stream of new life will delight God's Church, if one has truly achieved the social reign of the Sacred Heart in keeping with the revelation of Paray.[323] What treasures of sanctity, unexpected fruits of conversions are stored in the Most Sacred Heart, our joy and our highest hope, for those priests who apply themselves to making It known and loved by mankind, without faint-heartedness or human respect; who are ready to live completely and forever with Him, by Him and for Him, in an intimate partnership of ideals, interests, and sacrifices, without fear of obstacles or of contradiction! "I have never given God anything but love," said St. Thérèse of the Child Jesus, "and He will repay me with love."[324]

Oh, how much it means to me to convince the servants of Jesus Christ to set no other goal than the glorification of the Sacred Heart of Jesus! Just believe it; the advantage will be entirely yours. Do we lack talent, assistance and virtue? Take courage: "He is the treasure of the real poor."[325] Are we full of spiritual needs? "He is the inexhaustible source of all goods, in which love causes us to find

---

[321] "Never is love for God inactive; for it brings forth great things if it is present, but if it has stopped working, then there is no love left either" (St. Gregory the Great, *Homilia XXX in Evangelia: Habita ad populum in basilica sancti Petri apostoli die sancto Pentecostae* [Jn. 14:23-31], II, 2; PL 76, 1221).

[322] "You shall receive an hundred times as much" (Mk. 10:30).

[323] We deliberately say the *reign of the Heart of Jesus and not the reign of Jesus Christ*, so as to point out by our choice of words the fact that Jesus wants to reign through love.

[324] St. Thérèse of the Child Jesus, *Story of a Soul*, chapter 11.

[325] St. Margaret Mary, II, 232.

everything that we need."[326] Do we fear that we have lost all right to heaven's grace? Yet "He is a hidden, infinite treasure, who desires only to reveal Himself to us, to pour Himself out and to distribute Himself, so as to enrich our poverty."[327]

How much I wish that I could make young priests—especially these—lead a life of intimacy with the Divine Heart, which in all the tabernacles of the world is languishing for love and looks at the fields that are already ripe for the harvest and at the small number of true laborers. "The little ones have asked for bread, and there was none to break it for them."[328]

How gladly would I give my life so that they might resolve to consecrate to this extremely gentle Heart of the Redeemer *explicitly* and *irrevocably* all that they are and have, all that they can do and hope, their person, their life, their studies, their activity, the souls entrusted to them, their preaching, the tedious and difficult service of hearing confessions, their spiritual care for the sick and the numerous forms of their divine mission. Undertaken with Him and for Him, their adoration would be more profound, their prayers more zealous, their thanksgivings fuller, their pleading more ardent, their prostrations more effective. In that way though would merit "the friendship and the eternal blessings of this lovable Heart".[329]

---

[326] St. Margaret Mary, II, 381.

[327] St. Margaret Mary, II, 405.

[328] Cf. Lam. 4:4.

[329] St. Margaret Mary, II, 427. I take the liberty of bringing to the attention of priests who devote themselves to pastoral work a little transaction with which I have had success. When I hear the confession of penitents who receive communion often, I tell them, as their only penance or as an additional one, to receive Holy Communion on a particular day in honor of the Sacred Heart of Jesus, in order to obtain a particular grace that I note mentally or, if prudence does not prevent me, that I describe to them in more detail. Besides the extraordinary glory that these communions give to the Sacred Heart of Jesus, and the advantage in giving this important act a precise purpose—which the penitents would almost never do on their own initiative—one can picture the practical usefulness of this custom for the shepherds and the parish. Imagine a hardened sinner who one morning had to fight against fifty or a hundred communions that are being offered to the Sacred Heart of Jesus for his conversion!

"Our whole life must be directed toward this union with the Sacred Heart of our King through a pure, simple act, ... through the union of will, ... through one's mind and actions."[330] And then, yes then He will place at our disposal the value of His merits, the power of His Blood, the efficacy of His grace *ut fructificemus Deo.*[331] In this way our love becomes a continual Holy Mass, every one of us becomes in a twofold respect priest and victim with Him who is the sacrificial Victim par excellence and the eternal High Priest: *veritatem... facientes in caritate, crescamus in illo per omnia qui est caput, Christo.*[332]

Oh yes, let us stay closely united with Jesus by keeping awake in our hearts the passion for His glory and a hunger for His justice. Everything apart from Him is vanity. *Ad quem ibimus? Verba vitae aeternae habes.*[333] Let us live by Him, as the branch lives by the grapevine; let loving Him without measure be the measure of our love! Let the progressive fusion of our will with His be the foundation and plan for our holiness! Let speaking about Him always, everywhere and in every way be the secret of our strength, the glorious hallmark of our apostolate![334]

If we persevere in love, as He has admonished us, then at the same time we will remain in joy, peace, truth and life. Everything will be blessed, purified and transformed in Him and through Him; with Him everything will be sanctified and deified. Our life, identified with His, will become a continual Amen and an

---

[330] St. Margaret Mary, II, 419

[331] "That we may bring forth fruit to God" (Rom. 7:4).

[332] "Doing the truth in charity, we may in all things grow up in him who is the head, even Christ" (Eph. 4:15).

[333] "To whom shall we go? Thou hast the words of eternal life" (Jn. 6:69).

[334] Since I consecrated my life to the purpose of making priests acquainted with the Sacred Heart of Jesus, I constantly receive letters from my "converts" who express their astonishment and their grateful joy. "Oh, if I had known this sooner!" they write. "I do not recognize myself! I have become a new man! My parish is transformed! I am living in trust! I receive everything that I ask for from the Sacred Heart of Jesus! My interior life has taken a new direction; I would have never believed it, etc." And I answer them—trusting in our Lord's word: "*Modicae fidei, quare dubitasti? Majus videbis!* "O thou of little faith, why didst thou doubt? Greater things than these shalt thou see" (Mt. 14:31; Jn. 1:50).

uninterrupted Alleluia. "He ardently desires that this devotion be spread to all hearts, so that he might reign absolutely in them."[335]

Do we really want to save souls? Well then good, precisely for the sake of this goal He willed to reveal His Heart to the world: *Ut salvetur mundus per ipsum ... ut omnis qui credit in eum non pereat, sed habeat vitam aeternam.*[336]

Pertransiit Benefaciendo[337]

We want to take a closer look also at the promises of Jesus to those who honor His Sacred Heart. They are great, regal, magnificent, and at the same time clear, explicit, precisely delineated, historically certain, as His saintly confidante communicated them to us with anxious fidelity and candid innocence. She herself said: "How could I not relate everything about this lovable devotion and tell the whole world about the treasures and graces that Jesus Christ contains in His adorable Heart and is willing to pour out abundantly on all who will only practice this devotion?"[338]

With what an ardent soul the clergy should meditate on these promises! With what simplicity they should believe them! For to believe in them is to pay honor to the infinite love that dictated them, so that they may be an effective revelation of God's Heart: *Qui in Christum credis, et ejus crede sermonibus.*[339] How carefully and how urgently one should preach these promises, teach them, spread them, for they are designed to relieve so many bodily and mental ills and to mitigate so many sufferings that fill the heart with sorrow!

Meditate first on how all-encompassing they are. We can say that all categories of individual human beings and all social classes are assured of special graces: sinners, the lukewarm, the zealous, those beset by temptations, the downcast, those who are well, the sick, those who are occupied with business,

---

[335] St. Margaret Mary, II, 311.

[336] "That the world may be saved by him... that whosoever believeth in him may not perish, but may have life everlasting" (Jn. 3:16-17).

[337] "[He] went about doing good" (Acts 10:38).

[338] St. Margaret Mary, I, 141; II, 626.

[339] "You who believe in Christ, believe also His preachers" (St. Jerome, *Epistolae secundum ordinem temporum XIV ad Heliodorum monachum,* 1; PL 22, 348).

those who work for the salvation of souls, households, families, religious communities, nations, rulers, the whole world.... *Dives in omnes qui invocant illum!* [340]

Finally, meditate on how our Lord in His wisdom weighed His words, and reflect that He will keep His word—He, who with these promises pledged His honor, the honor of a God! Moreover He calls Himself the Faithful One,[341] the Almighty;[342] *pius promissor, fidelis redditor, indefessus adjutor.*[343]

Do not neglect either to take into consideration the generosity of the Giver, which becomes evident through these unconditional, unlimited and unstinting gifts. He promises the necessary graces according to each one's state in life and the circumstances of the moment; and by that He has in mind *all* the graces that one might need. He promises to console all who sorrow, in *all* their griefs; He blesses *all* the undertakings of those who honor Him; He has in store for sinners the treasures of mercy and for the just—a swift and lofty perfection; He assures priests of the priceless gift of converting hearts—*all* hearts, note well, *even the most hardened....* Tell me, could our misery hope for more? And could almighty Goodness oblige Itself any more extensively? *Quodcumque*

---

[340] "Rich unto all that call upon him" (Rom. 10:12). As for nations and rulers, France is mentioned directly in the revelation of Paray, but we may suppose that other nations by analogy have a share in this promise. Cf. August Hamon, S.J., *Message du Sacré-Coeur à Louis XIV, à la France: Étude historique et critique* [The Message of the Sacred Heart to Louis XIV and France: Historical and critical study] (Paris: Gabriel Beauchesne, 1918); Ernest Truptin, *Le drapeau du Sacré-Coeur et la Bienheureuse Marguerite-Marie* [The Banner of the Sacred Heart and Blessed Margaret Mary] (Autun: Imprimerie Notre-Dame des Anges, 1918); François Veuillot, *Le drapeau [national] du Sacré-Coeur* [The national flag of the Sacred Heart of Jesus] (Paris: Tolra, 1899).

[341] Cf. Apoc. 19:11.

[342] Gen. 17:1

[343] "The loving promiser, the faithful restorer, the untiring helper" (*Epistola seu tractatus ad fratres de Monte Dei,* a treatise once attributed to St. Bernard of Clairvaux, but considered today to be the work of William of Saint-Thierry, a friend of St. Bernard, or sometimes to D. Guigon, the fifth General Superior of the Carthusians; cf. PL 184, 298 and 307; 180, 206; 153, 590).

petieritis Patrem in nomine meo, hoc faciam.[344] Therefore trust in Him, thank Him for the signs of favor that He has granted you, so as to merit new ones, *plenissime sciens, quia quaecumque promisit, potens est et facere.*[345]

Narrow-mindedness and fears, dangerous adventures beset us on every side: *A Domino corripimur, ut non cum hoc mundo damnemur.*[346] Oh, how consoling it should be for us to be able to present to dejected souls the great lavishness of the divine promises, evangelizare *investigabiles divitias Christi!*[347]

How consistent with love, how humane it is to remind someone who laments the humiliation of a defeat that "the most effective means of lifting us up again after a fall is the Sacred Heart of our Lord Jesus Christ"![348] How wonderful it is to explain to someone who is sorrowing and weeping, that "all bitterness whatsoever is sweetness in this adorable Heart, where everything is transformed into love"![349] How Christian it is to teach someone who trembles at the thought of eternity that "a child cannot be lost in the arms of an almighty Father who wants us to pay our debts with the treasures of His Sacred Heart."[350]

But what would happen to us if by our deliberate, ongoing opposition, our daily infidelities and our habitual apathy we made ourselves unworthy of sharing in the great triumph of mercy?

The "Author of life"[351] is the one who said this: *Unigenitus Filius qui est in sinu Patris, ipse enarravit.*[352] Woe to him who believes that he is self-sufficient and rejects the gifts of God!

---

[344] "Whatsoever you shall ask the Father in my name, that will I do" (Jn. 14:13).

[345] "Most fully knowing [i.e. fully convinced] that whatsoever [God] has promised, he is able also to perform (Rom. 4:21).

[346] "We are chastised by the Lord, that we be not condemned with this world" (1Cor. 12:32; cf. Heb. 12:6).

[347] "To preach ... the unsearchable riches of Christ" (Eph. 3:8).

[348] St. Margaret Mary, II, 159.

[349] St. Margaret Mary, II, 235, 473.

[350] St. Margaret Mary, II, 386, 411, 135, 722, 52, 108.

[351] Acts 3:15.

[352] "The only begotten Son who is in the bosom of the Father, he hath declared him" (Jn. 1:18).

God grant that there be only few such unfortunate souls! ...
*Confiteor tibi Pater, quia abscondisti haec a sapientibus et prudentibus,
et revelasti ea parvulis.*[353]

In Hoc Signo Vinces![354]

Let us meditate now in a special way on the image of the
divine Heart. Our divine Savior wants this image to be the object
of love, respect, honor, profound reverence and ardent, confident
entreaties. Have we, I ask, always propagated this image zealously,
with conviction and enthusiasm?

Oh, what an adorable image of the Sacred Heart of Jesus,
the strength of our souls, the ineffable delight of our poor heart!
How plainly and exactly does it symbolize and remind us of the
whole familiar, gentle story of the love of the incarnate God! How
effectively it summarizes His care, His admonitions, preaching and
invitations, His boundless amiability and His infinite love![355]

How mighty it is in appeasing heaven's wrath! It is like the
blood of the lamb on the doorposts of the Hebrews: The angel of

---

[353] "I confess to thee [i.e. praise thee], O Father, ... because thou hast hid
these things from the wise and prudent and hast revealed them to little
ones" (Mt. 11:25; Lk. 10:21).

[354] In this sign you will conquer!

[355] The Angelic Doctor instructs us that our nature does not allow us to
lift ourselves up to God through knowledge and love without the help of a
perceptible object (St. Thomas Aquinas, *Summa Contra Gentiles*, III, 119).
In another passage he maintains that sensory things are not only necessary
for us in order to recognize divine things, but also in order to love them.
From this he concludes that the humanity of Jesus Christ and all that is
related to it is splendidly effective in leading us to devotion (St. Thomas
Aquinas, *Summa Theologiae*, II-II, q. 83, art. 3, ad 2).
Throughout this chapter I wish to speak about the images in which
Jesus shows His Heart. These are the only images of the Sacred Heart
of Jesus that are permitted for public worship (*Sacra Rituum Congregatio*,
Decrees of 4 April 1879 and 28 August 1891). Nevertheless, pictures in
which the Sacred Heart appears without the person of Jesus are worthy
of the worship of *latria* just like the first sort, and they are permitted for
personal devotion (cf. St. Thomas Aquinas, *Summa Theologiae*, III, q. 25,
art. 3 and 4).

justice who descended to earth as the bearer of death sees it, adores it and passes over, for wherever Jesus rules as supreme Lord, God's forgiveness descends more abundantly and generously.

How much our gentle Redeemer wishes to see this image distributed to children in their catechism classes, ... bequeathed as a sacred treasure in all families, ... honored with solemn worship in all churches, ... surrounded by tender love in convents, seminaries, colleges and schools, ... posted in stores and workshops, in prisons and courtrooms, wherever people work, pray, suffer or weep, *ut sit in omnibus ipse primatum tenens!*[356]

We must truly be convinced of it: "He takes special pleasure in being honored in this depiction of His Heart of flesh, and He wishes that this image be carried in public so as to touch the senseless hearts of the people."[357]

Who can tell the holy thoughts that it awakens, the sweet memories that it calls to mind, the splendid, immediate effects that it produces? The utmost consolation amid the fears of the soul, a sweet glimpse of paradise, an incentive for the faithful, generous performance of duty—which is the most genuine and surest form of any sanctity. This image shares in the miraculous power of the divine Redeemer: *Virtus de illo exibat, et sanabat omnes.*[358]

After a long series of infidelities or in the tormenting pangs of conscience from a recent fall, in the indescribable agony of a desecrated soul that would like to tear itself away from the demeaning slavery of the senses, in the terrible trembling of human dignity that strives in vain to lift itself up, in the horrible darkness of sin, ... the image of the Sacred Heart arises! These flames, this light, this Blood, this adorable Face... and automatically a sanctifying cry is wrung from the soul: *Jesu, fili David, miserere mei!*[359]

If we find ourselves subject to the seductive charm of creatures, in the humiliating, painful rebellions of sensuality, in those moments when the deceptive attraction of forbidden pleasure seems to triumph over reason and faith, let us fix our gaze on the Sacred Heart! ... It loves us so much! Reflect on how much It

---

[356] "That in all things he may hold the primacy" (Col. 1:18).

[357] St. Margaret Mary, I, 244.

[358] "Virtue went out from him and healed all" (Lk. 6:19).

[359] "Jesus, Son of David, have mercy on me" (Mk. 10:47).

suffered for you! ... Despite everything, hold fast..., reflect, ... only a moment, ... draw new strength, ... resist ... at least for His love's sake! Oh, yes, *Domine, salva nos, perimus!*[360]

When the soul is afflicted by a deep sorrow, crushed to the ground under the weight of a large, oppressive, undeserved cross, ... in the nightmare of near-despair, when in the depths a hatred of mankind, the need for revenge seethes, the foolish desire of the blood..., oh then stop and look up! See the Heart of Him who loves, forgives, forgets and blesses. He can bring healing for everything, ... He is able and willing to save you... *Ego sum, nolite timere!*[361]

In how many unhappy, guilt-ridden souls has this sacred image reawakened the awareness of their duty! How many has it kept back, as though by a miracle, from the brink of the abyss! How many has it helped to find again the path of virtue and rekindled in them like a sacred fire an endless nostalgia for heaven! This image is the center of a special devotion, it is a very effective means of recruiting Catholics and not the deceptive image of a shrieking satanic hatred; it is the object of the most tender advantages of divine love; neither heaven nor earth, nor hell itself, can resist its gentle influence, its happy radiance of mercy, compassion and love: *Gratias Deo super inenarrabili dono ejus!*[362]

Let us then make images of the adorable Heart fall like a shower of roses[363] on this careless, sensual society, for It wants to redeem it,

---

[360] "Lord, save us, we perish" (Mt. 8:25).

[361] "It is I. Be not afraid" (Jn. 6:20).

[362] "Thanks be to God for his unspeakable gift" (2Cor. 9:15).

[363] St. Thérèse of the Child Jesus used to say: "I will spend my heaven doing good on earth. After my death I will make a shower of roses fall on the earth" (*Story of a Soul*, chapter 12).

Of course this is not a matter of tossing around countless copies of this image, so to speak. They must be distributed according to the dictates of prudence, and we must till the soil that is to receive the seed of moral restoration, proclaim the favorable moment, allow the hour of grace to mature by prayer, and surround with care the families in which this blessed sign has been successfully introduced.... To act otherwise could give the appearance of superstition. One might also accuse us of tempting God, who demands of us a *rationabile obsequium* [service in keeping with reason] (Rom. 12:1). Moreover we run the risk of giving scandal to the weak and spoiling the reputation of this divinely-willed practice, which is and let us trust: *Si credideris, videbis gloriam Dei.*[364]

Finally and above all—*rogamus et obsecramus vos in Domino Jesu*[365]—no priest should be so little concerned about his own spiritual interests, so indifferent to the welfare of souls, that he neglects to set up in his own residence, in a place visible to all, a large, impressive image of this divine Heart that has loved mankind so much. Is life hard, oppressive and worse than death? Well, good: *curramus ad propositum nobis certamen, aspicientes in … Jesum.*[366]

But why—I have often asked myself—should the rectory alone be absent from this universal crusade of faith and love that is so enthusiastically encouraged by the Church, and be the only place excluded from these divine blessings that Jesus has reserved according to His promise to those houses in which His image is honored?

Let us have faith, you shepherds of souls, in the Heart of Him who is the *princeps pastorum;*[367] let us finally believe in His love, in His words, which are *spirit* and *life*[368], and He will make it His duty to satisfy our pious wishes as well as the holy ambition of our priestly soul: *Qui credit in me, non sitiet unquam.*[369]

---

nonetheless the highest hope of good priests.

[364] "If thou believe, thou shalt see the glory of God" (Jn. 11:40).

[365] "We pray and beseech you in the Lord Jesus" (1 Thess. 4:1).

[366] Let us run by patience to the fight proposed to us, looking on Jesus" (Heb. 12:1-2).

[367] "The prince of pastors" (1 Pet. 5:4).

[368] Jn. 6:64.

[369] "He that believeth in me shall never thirst" (Jn. 6:35). I take the liberty of recalling that God *licet sit magnus in magnis, mirabilia tamen gloriosius operatur in minimis* [Although God is great in His great saints, He nevertheless works even more glorious miracles in His least ones]. (Office of the Holy Innocents, Pope Leo I the Great, *Liber Sacramentorum, XLII: In natali innocentium, 2;* PL 55, 152 C; optional prayer for the Feast of the Holy Innocents: *Deus qui licet sis magnus in magnis, mirabilia tamen gloriosius operaris in minimis, da nobis, quaesumus, in eorum celebritate audere, qui Filio tuo Domino nostro testimonium praebuerunt etiam non loquentes* [O God, although You are great in Your great saints, You nevertheless work even more glorious miracles in Your least ones; grant us, we pray, to be bold on the feast of those who even as infants bore witness to Your Son, our Lord]. This prayer is found also in the 1754 *Vetus missale romanum*

In Cruce Salus[370]

No, no, do not tell me, "the Cross is enough for me, for this too shows us Jesus and speaks about His infinite love; moreover it is the official, traditional representation in the Church of God." I beg you, do not pit one devotion against another.

These two forms of Christian iconography, whose historical developments are so closely connected, can and should continue side by side like the two different devotional forms of which they are the happy expression. After all, they are not designed to be mutually exclusive, but rather complementary.[371] No, we have not undertaken an iconoclastic propaganda campaign in God's name and at His commend, but rather a pious crusade that intends to glorify Jesus and cannot and will not set aside the likeness of the Man of Sorrows. Genuine Christianity must necessarily put down its roots in the Blood of Calvary, this ineffable bath of restoration and life, but tell me, is this not the Blood of the Sacred Heart of Jesus?

Moreover the divine teacher knew that the Church surrounds the cross with great honor, and yet, without excluding or rejecting one or another devotion, He commissioned St. Margaret Mary to preach His meek Heart as the purest expression of Christianity,

---

monasticum lateranense [Old Roman Missal of the Lateran monks] as a special prayer for the feast day at Vespers.) God has been pleased in recent years to work the most splendid miracles solely by means of the simple invocation: *Heart of Jesus, I place my trust in You!* This is pointed out by St. Margaret Mary also: "Often great graces are connected with something that seems small to us" (II, 662).

If this invocation is prayed fifty or one hundred times in the form of a novena, while counting them on the beads of a rosary, it is enough to obtain great trust for souls of little faith, to reform a miserable human being, or to convert the most hardened hearts. Here again I can only say: Try it, and you will see!

[370] In the Cross is salvation.

[371] The reader can consult Thomas, Desjardins, Barenton and also the find depictions that Paranque and Richstätter have left us in their books. Most of all, though, I recommend the work by Fr. Auguste Hamon, S.J., *Histoire de la Dévotion au Sacré-Coeur,* 5 vols. (Paris: Gabriel Beauchesne, 1923-1940), and in this context in vol. 2, *L'Aube de la dévotion* [The Beginning of the Devotion] (Paris, 1925), the chapter entitled *"Iconographie du Sacré-Coeur",* 319-353.

as the most eloquent and effective sign of His affection for souls. In fact "this Heart full of love suffered more than all the rest of Jesus' sacred humanity."[372] It enables us to delve more deeply into the mysteries of Divine Love, it allows us to put our finger on the innermost reasons for the terrible drama, *sanguinis sacramentum*,[373] which redeemed the human race and concluded with the wounding of this Sacred Heart.

Affer manum tuam, our Lord said to the Apostle Thomas, *et mitte in latus meum et noli esse incredulus, sed fidelis.*[374] We too want to fix our gaze on this pierced Heart; then we will understand better the reason for so many sufferings which, considered in themselves, were by no means necessary for the salvation of the world, *in finem dilexit.*[375] Our Lord willed it so and so must anyone who boasts of being His servant: *Qui habet mandata mea et servat ea, ille est qui diligit me.*[376]

But let us assume for the moment that He had not commanded so insistently the propagation of this adorable image. Even then, having this image before our eyes and making it our delight would really have to be for us priests a tenderly urgent necessity, a heart-felt need, for (and this is a well-known psychological phenomenon) one does not really love a person whom one does not keep in mind. Then too, one seldom thinks of someone whose picture one does not honor although one could do so.[377]

Let us therefore put a beautiful image of the Sacred Heart on our desk, so as to be able to look at it often; let us put it in our breviary, so that it accompanies us everywhere: *esse cum Jesu, dulcis Paradisus.*[378] Let us entrust to Him our troubles, let us ask for His

---

[372] St. Margaret Mary, II, 556.

[373] The sacrament of the Blood (St. Jerome, *Commentaria in Evangelium Matthaei ad Eusebium,* III [Mt 16:20]; PL 26, 118).

[374] "Bring hither thy hand and put it into my side. And be not faithless, but believing" (Jn. 20:27).

[375] "He loved them unto the end" (Jn. 13:1). St. Thomas clearly says that love alone can explain the unprecedented sufferings of our Lord (St. Thomas Aquinas, *Summa Theologiae,* III, q. 47, art. 3).

[376] "He that hath my commandments and keepeth them; he it is that loveth me" (Jn. 14:21).

[377] Cf. St. Thomas Aquinas, *Summa Theologiae,* I-II, q. 48, art. 2, ad 2.

[378] "To be with Jesus is a delightful heaven" (Thomas à Kempis, *The Imitation of Christ,* Book II, Chapter 8).

counsel in our doubts, consolation in bitterness, light in darkness, strength in temptations...; let us console Him by our generous promises; let us speak to him in confidence those ardent words that love inspires in us; let us cover Him often with passionate kisses: He is our treasure, our blessedness, our glory, our hope, *ut sive vigilemus, sive dormiamus, simul cum illo vivamus.*[379]

Lux in Tenebris Lucet[380]

Servant of the Lord, look around, look near and far: Everything tells you that a bloody storm has swept across the world, *sunt lacrymae rerum*;[381] but at the same time you can discern everywhere signs that a resurrection is drawing near: *Levate capita vestra, quoniam appropinquat redemptio vestra.*[382]

Leo XIII wrote with his golden pen: "When the Church, in the days immediately succeeding her institution, was oppressed beneath the yoke of the Caesars, a young Emperor saw in the heavens a cross, which became at once the happy omen and cause of the glorious victory that soon followed. And now, today, behold another blessed and heavenly token is offered to our sight: the most Sacred Heart of Jesus, with a cross rising from it and shining forth with dazzling splendor amidst flames of love. In that Sacred Heart all our hopes should be placed, and from it the salvation of men is to be confidently besought."[383]

More than thirty years have passed since that day, and you can joyfully observe what fundamental transformations have taken

---

[379] "[So] that whether we watch or sleep, we may live together with him" (1 Thess. 5:10). It goes without saying that the image is a *means* and not an *end*. It is supposed to remind us of the living Heart in the tabernacle and keep us very close to it in our thoughts, even when we are physically far away from it. All signs of honor that we pay to the image are naturally referred to the real, living Heart in heaven and "under the Eucharistic species, these incomparable signs that simultaneously conceal and loudly proclaim His love" (Charles *Sauvé, L'Eucharistie intime: Élévations Dogmatiques* [Intimacy with the Eucharist: Dogmatic reflections], 2 vols. [Paris: J. de Gigord, 1919], 1:334).

[380] "The light shineth in darkness" (Jn. 1:5).

[381] "There are tears in things." (Virgil, Aeneid, Book 1, verse 462).

[382] "Lift up your heads, because your redemption is at hand" (Lk. 21:28).

[383] Leo XIII, Encyclical *Annum Sacrum* (25 May 1899), par. 12.

place in the world under the salutary influence of this "blessed and heavenly token". One commentator wrote that "we are experiencing a *new Pentecost*, destined to warm the world in the flames of the Sacred Heart of Jesus", and we may already repeat, in truth, what the confidante of the Heart of Jesus said in her artless simplicity: "The foe is bursting with rage, because he could not prevent [the spread of] this marvelous devotion."[384] One must admit that "this salutary means has already snatched many souls away from him and will snatch from him many, many more."[385] It is very consoling that a flourishing of holy organizations and good works followed the bleak madness of destruction that covered this poor Europe with outrage for five whole years,[386] and we are allowed to hope that Divine Providence is preparing new, pleasant surprises for us: Certainly God's hour is not far off.[387]

Jesus proclaimed this in the middle of His ignominious Passion: *Rex sum ego*,[388] and the angels of peace, borne up by this soaring hope, seem to sing to those of good will: *Oportet illum regnare.*[389] The angels sing it as the prophets once sang it; and the Supreme Shepherd showed the dawn of new ages to the Church, which trembled for joy at it, by instituting the solemn feast of Christ the King, which in a certain sense is the *social kingship of the Sacred Heart of Jesus.* We would gladly speak about the joyful memory of an accomplished fact; at least it is unshakable trust in the divine promises: *Pater, venit hora, clarifica Filium tuum.*[390]

These *Concordats* which put an end to lamentable abuses and secure "tranquility in order";[391] the creation of new representations and legations to the Holy See, the diplomatic relations of the various states with the Vatican, which have become more cordial, the more respectful attitude of governments toward the Successor of Peter, a respect that leads minds to make reparation for all their errors—

---

[384] St. Margaret Mary, II, 620.

[385] St. Margaret Mary, II, 340.

[386] The reference is to World War I, 1914-1918.

[387] These lines were written in 1930.

[388] "Thou sayest that [i.e. Yes,] I am a king" (Jn. 18:37).

[389] "He must reign" (1Cor. 15:25).

[390] "Father, the hour is come. Glorify thy Son" (Jn. 17:1).

[391] *"Tranquillitas ordinis"* (St. Augustine, *De Civitate Dei,* Part II, Book 19, Chapter 13.1; PL 41, 640).

all this is a solemn lesson and a reason for gladness.[392] Mankind, cleansed by a bloodbath, is setting a new course.

While mankind weeps before the One who gladly forgives,[393] and after the fall of almost forty thrones, with the definitive abandonment of so many regimes, in the stormy disappearance of many, many ideals, in this sad world that was thought to be on the eve of anarchy, we are on the brink of the achievement of the great event: "'What do you fear? I will reign....'[394] Yes, this amiable Heart will reign, despite Satan! This saying fills me with joy and thoroughly consoles me."[395]

And you try to answer with the cold words of doubting Thomas: *Nisi videro, non credam.*[396]

Nisi videris?! [Unless you see?!] Listen! In November 1902 the Freemasons posted on the walls in Paris a clearly worded manifesto that testified blasphemously in the devil's language to the glories and renown of the Sacred Heart of Jesus. [The caricature showed] a monstrous night owl, whose features resembled those of the Most Reverend Cardinal Archbishop Richard, covering with his big black wings the Basilica of Montmartre. The church, which is dedicated to the Sacred Heart of Jesus, appeared to be radiant with light, while he cast the thickest darkness on the capital spread out at his feet, and on the rest of the world. Beneath the blasphemous picture the viewer could read the mean insult: *Voilà l'ennemi* ["This is the enemy!"].[397]

---

[392] After World War I at least 32 states maintained diplomatic relations with the Holy See; 27 governments had an embassy at the Vatican and 25 granted papal representatives the right of hospitality. Cf. Auguste Hamon, S.J., *"Chronique du mouvement religieux"* [Chronicle of the Religious Movement] in: *Études* (published by the Jesuit Fathers, Paris) 63/189 (1926): 616. It is almost unnecessary to recall the reconciliation of the Supreme Shepherd with the Italian government.

[393] Dante, *Divine Comedy, Purgatorio,* Canto 3, first section, verses 119-120. "There, weeping, I commended my soul / To the Judge who gladly grants pardon."

[394] St. Margaret Mary, II, 537.

[395] St. Margaret Mary, II, 436.

[396] "Except [i.e. unless] I shall see... I will not believe" (Jn. 20:25).

[397] Cf. Mgr. Henri Louis Odelin, *Le Cardinal Richard, 1819-1908:* Souvenirs (Paris: J. de Gigord, 1922); Mgr. Maurice Clément, *Vie du Cardinal Richard, archevêque de Paris* (Paris: J. de Gigord, 1924).

What do you think about that? Do you remember the episode of the demoniacs of Gerasa? *Quid nobis et tibi, Jesu? ... venisti huc ante tempus torquere nos?*[398]

What do you say to that? That hellish sect understood—and to what an extent, my God!—that mankind finds salvation in the Most Sacred Heart of Jesus.... And you, the "Anointed of the Lord", stubbornly refuse to understand it!

But I can tell you still more! Probably you don't know it, but the heretics themselves "believe in love", trust in the adorable Heart of the incarnate Word and surround it with honor and affection. For more than fifty years there have been in the Anglican churches of Europe and America side chapels, images and statutes of the Sacred Heart of Jesus, and even among these apostates one finds traces of a modest apologetic and ascetical literature on this topic. The Protestant association "For the Union of Churches"—a very extensive association—professes this blessed devotion without any human respect.[399] It is humbling but undeniable: *Fas est et ab hoste doceri*! ["It is salutary to be instructed even by one's enemy."]

What else should I say? Just look around! Knock at the gates of the splendid palaces, which all too often open to the idols of the age and to every demeaning shame of the flesh; look at all the families that are known to be religiously indifferent or even enemies of the Cross of Christ; go into the workshops where man becomes a machine or a mere number: set foot in the dismal nooks and crannies where stupefaction and misery reign as supreme mistress; pitch your tent amid the dregs of society, where life usually plays out in incomparable sorrows and nameless crimes... *leva in circuitu oculos tuos et vide!*[400] Everywhere heads are bowed and knees are bent before the symbol of divine love, and we find hearts and lips that sing their Hosanna to this Love: *publicani et meretrices crediderunt ei.*[401]

And you, who thanks to His goodness take your place among the princes of His people, you who make the angels envious,

---

[398] "What have we to do with thee, Jesus? ... Art thou come hither to torment us before the time?" (Mt. 8:29).

[399] Cf. Paul Thureau-Dangin, *La renaissance catholique en Angleterre au 19e siècle*, 3 vols. (Paris: Plon-Nourrit, 1899-1906).

[400] "Lift up thy eyes round about and see" (Isa. 60:4).

[401] "The publicans and the harlots believed him" (Mt. 21:32).

you who judge and heal the leprosy of the soul, you who are the dispenser of His mysteries, *Dei consul factus,*[402] you who speak in His name and enjoy the reverence due Him and are the object of His tender loving care, *discipulus quem diligebat Jesus,*[403] you still wish to persist in your absurd opposition and irreverence? *An divitias bonitatis ejus, et patientiae, et longanimitatis contemnis?*[404] See how ill suited this is to the wonderful harmony of this comprehensive agreement. If you are not afraid to give scandal to the little ones and the lowly who believe in Him, you should know at least that the consequences of your incorrect, inexplicable attitude could be irremediable. *Secundum enim duritiam tuam et impoenitens cor, thesaurizas tibi iram in die irae.*[405]

Let us speak frankly: Do you not see, or are you unwilling to see? And you want to criticize? You want to condemn? And you claim to know better than the Church, the "pillar and ground of the truth"?[406] Listen to these words from the mouth of Jesus: *Si caeci essetis, non haberetis peccatum; nunc vero dicitis: quia vidimus! Peccatum vestrum manet.*[407]

---

[402] "Thou who hast become God's counselor" (inscription on the tomb of Gregory the Great).

[403] "That disciple ... whom Jesus loved" (Jn. 21:7).

[404] "Or despisest thou the riches of his goodness and patience and longsuffering?" (Rom. 2:4).

[405] "But according to thy hardness and impenitent heart, thou treasurest up to thyself wrath against the day of wrath" (Rom. 2:5).

[406] 1 Tim. 3:15.

[407] "If you were blind, you should not have sin: but now you say: We see. Your sin remaineth" (Jn. 9:41).

Three black men from Uganda, who had received their education and formation from the White Fathers and Bp. Lavigerie and were about to be ordained priests—Timotheus, Michael and Gregorius, poor sons of Ham—wrote on November 9, 1923, to an Italian priest, their great benefactor, these very words in good Latin: *Dominum incessanter exore ut det nobis cor docile et tenerrimum erga SS. Cor suum, ut semper magis ac magis exardescamus flagrantissimo ac potentissimo incendio amoris sui, ut eumdem caritatis ignem in animis fidelium excitare et fovere non cessemus.* ["Pray the Lord ceaselessly that He may give us a docile, tender heart toward His Most Sacred Heart, so that we may increasingly burn with this brightly-glowing, mighty fire of His love, and may never stop kindling and tending this same

The Miracle of Love

Nisi videris? [Unless you see?] After so many years of priestly ministry have you really not yet noticed that where the Sacred Heart of Jesus reigns, "the brightness of the Father's glory"[408] and the "Sun of justice",[409] the city of God, *amor Dei usque ad contemptum sui,* grows mightier and more extensive, while the city of Satan, *amor sui usque ad contemptum Dei,*[410] is weakened and totters?

Nisi videris? What more do you want to see? *Tu solus peregrinus es in Jerusalem?*[411]

The whole world is converted through the Sacred Heart of Jesus, *quod scimus loquimur, et quod vidimus testamur.*[412] An incredible flourishing of virtues and sanctity is becoming evident in all classes of society. The superhuman miracles of evangelical perfection have now become an everyday occurrence in the Church. Beatifications follow one another, their number increasing impressively in the last two centuries; in the annals of Catholicism this is a brand new chapter. This white-robed legion of sacrificial souls, pure as angels, countless as the stars of heaven, wants to imitate the heroic martyrs. They live on sacrifice and prayer, on humility and in peace, on silence and forgiveness. These are the unconquerable ranks of the religious communities that rose up after the Revolution stronger,

---

fire of charity in the souls of the faithful."] And Timotheus, meanwhile ordained a priest, wrote on December 28, 1924: *Verbi ministerio occupari, et pro SS. Cordis Jesu exaltatione insudare, mihi voluptas est.* ["Devoting myself to the ministry of the Word and toiling for the exaltation of the Sacred Heart of Jesus is my delight."] I confess that I shed tears over this letter, and while I looked at the photograph of the three African Levites and the characteristic features of their bronze-colored faces, I praised the work of grace that is able to raise up children of Abraham from stones—and what stones! The complaint of our Most Holy Redeemer came to mind: *Regina Austri surget in judicio!* ["The Queen of the South shall rise in judgment"] (Mt. 12:42).

[408] Heb. 1:3

[409] Mal. 4:2.

[410] (a) "Love of God to the point of despising oneself"; (b) "self-love to the point of despising God" (St. Augustine, *De Civitate Dei,* Part II, Book 14, Chapter 28; PL 41, 436).

[411] "Art thou only a stranger in Jerusalem?" (Lk. 24:18).

[412] "We speak what we know and we testify what we have seen" (Jn. 3:11).

more disciplined, more zealous, better loved and more hated than ever, so as to sum up in themselves the Catholic poetry of suffering and love, the passionate devotion to knowledge and the truth. Scholastic theology, renewed like an eagle in its youth,[413] is capable, under the leadership of the Angelic Doctor,[414] of continuing the glorious epic of the old battles and the pure traditions, so as to carry out new conquests of the mind with unshakable faith and new weapons. In thirty-seven Catholic universities human wisdom is wedded to the wisdom of God in order to fight the wickedness and injustices of error.[415] Then there are the sensational recantations and a whole-hearted return to the faith, leaving heresy, schism and godlessness behind. Here you see a hitherto unknown awakening of apostolic zeal and missionary propagation of the faith, which gladdens and consoles the heart of the Supreme Shepherd.... He is opposed by sterile machinations in the lodges, which are united in an international pact of destruction and death.... *Videtis quia nihil proficimus? Ecce totus mundus post eum abiit.*[416]

Nisi videris? Tell me, then: Are you not yet convinced by this general renewal of the faith, this continual springtime of piety? Are you not encouraged by this immense host of authors and scholars— the glorious, tireless vanguard of Christian culture? In all branches of human knowledge it victoriously leaves the ineradicable marks of the Christian genius. Are you left indifferent by this marvelous organization of Catholic youth which goes forth to conquer as a compact, admirable army in battle array under the beloved banner, "either Christ or death"? Does it say nothing to you, this quivering of new life that is appearing everywhere, which flows fruitfully from the depths of a renewed conscience, *ut divino Cordi Christi regis, debitus amor, et cultus, et imperium restituatur.*[417] Are you not

---

[413] Ps. 102:5.

[414] So Pius XI calls St. Thomas Aquinas in his Encyclical *Studiorem ducem* (29 June 1923)

[415] To the 35 that existed in 1927 we must add the University of Valparaiso in Chile and, in 1930, the University of Salzburg in Austria.

[416] "Do you see that we prevail nothing? Behold, the whole world is gone after him" (Jn. 12:19).

[417] "To restore to the Sacred Heart of Christ His sovereign rule and the love and worship due Him" (Pius XI, Encyclical *Ubi arcano Dei* [23 December 1922]).

moved by this mysterious movement of the poor "dry bones" that are preparing to "hear the voice of the Almighty",[418] so as to rise again tomorrow, purified by remorse, transformed in love, ready to give their blood and their lives for the *Jesus of love?*[419]

Open your eyes and see..., broaden your mind and look at this divine comedy, this impressive festival, this sublime poem of love that is granted as a response to love: *Dico enim vobis, quod multi reges et prophetae voluerunt videre quae vos videtis, et non viderunt.*[420] And if you understand that it is sinful to deny known truth, then set aside once and for all your old prejudices, your disparaging skepticism, your alleged difficulties: *Noli esse incredulus, sed fidelis.*[421]

Omnis Lingua Confiteatur[422]

Because Jesus at any rate is not content with a simple, polite acceptance of His infallible word, in your judgment, and He has the right to demand of His priests at least a vigorous faith, made up of great ideals and generous enthusiasm, follow me a little further, and I will tell you, like the angel in the Apocalypse: *Veni et vide!*[423]

Every work that comes from God usually displays three signs of credibility: contradiction, fruitfulness, and dedication. Is this the case also with the Heart of Jesus? I leave it to you to decide.

CONTRADICTION! *Veni et Vide...*

For two centuries now the infinite love of the Redeemer has been in a gigantic battle with the wickedness or the careless indifference of mankind. Hell is mobilized to destroy, and Jesus works to build up anew. The *slaughter of the innocent children* is repeated every day in the schools, onstage in theaters, in the

---

[418] Cf. Ezec. 37:4.

[419] An expression frequently used by St. Catharine of Siena.

[420] "I say to you that many prophets and kings have desired to see the things that you see and have not seen them" (Lk. 10:24).

[421] "Be not faithless, but believing" (Jn. 20:27).

[422] "Let every tongue confess" (cf. Phil. 2:11).

[423] "Come and see" (Apoc. 6:1).

public squares in the name of a godless culture, under the pretext of hygiene, science, art or politics. And Jesus, who victoriously marches past these prejudices, past the difficulties of habit, draws the little ones every day to His Heart, which is the source and sanctuary of infinite love. Godlessness unceasingly desecrates and tears apart home life; it attacks the indissolubility of the bond of matrimony, weakens paternal authority and even endangers the transmission of life.

And Jesus, who wants to rule over families as Supreme Lord, draws them to Himself, one after the other, through the gentle attraction of His adorable Heart.... The Protestants' money buys consciences, which are infected and wholly influenced by rationalism, while the Church unwaveringly fights error in the name of Jesus Christ and proves day after day to be more than the sole administrator of sound doctrine and the infallible teacher of truth. These battles were foreseen by our Lord when He declared to the saintly Visitation nun with the certainty and exactitude of someone who reads the future: "He will rule despite His enemies."[424]

FRUITFULNESS! *Veni et Vide...*

Two centuries full of magnificence and triumphs, full of miracles and more and more great deeds of almighty love on behalf of misery that seeks help. It is divine fidelity, which divinely keeps its infallible promises; it is a sublime *Concordat* between the Sacred Heart of Jesus and mankind. This lovable Heart receives every day more loving affection, more tender reverence, more resolute and sincere love, more comprehensive honors, an ever increasing enthusiasm, a trust that knows no bounds.... *Principem et Salvatorem Deus exaltavit.*[425]

In all regions of the world there are hearts that beat, souls that quiver and—in a sublime outburst, with ardent conviction and with a unanimous, solemn act of thanksgiving to boundless Goodness—pay honor to the Heart of Jesus, *Moestorum consolatio, laborantium fortitudo.*[426] There are thousands—what am I saying?—millions

---

[424] St. Margaret Mary, I, 118; II, 489 – I, 97; II, 426 – I, 100; II, 436.

[425] "Him hath God exalted... to be Prince and Saviour" (Acts 5:31).

[426] "The consolation of the troubled, the strength of the suffering" (*Missale*

upon millions of believers who have found in it a strength against every weakness, a light against every darkness, infinite tenderness in abandonment, however sad, sudden liberation in every danger, however hidden and frightening it may be. It is a sweet fragrance and a joyful hymn of adoration and faith that rises, borne up by thanksgiving and praise.

DEDICATION! *Veni et Vide...*

The glorious series of twenty popes—do you understand?—a whole legion of saintly bishops, countless as the grains of sand on the seashore, and thirty International Eucharistic Congresses in their grandiose glory have set about studying, celebrating, defending, promoting, and recommending this devotion, which is so *attractive and so human*,[427] and have used every possible means to establish it. They have maintained and proclaimed, expressly and formally, that there is nothing dearer to our Lord or more beneficial for souls. Nothing is better suited to the spiritual needs and the yearning of our era, which has lost the idea of true beauty and has blasphemously falsified love.[428]

Must I go on about these things at greater length? As you see, the premises of the syllogism prove to be perfectly true; hence the conclusion is legitimate also, namely that this is a work of God: *Deo... gratias, qui dedit nobis victoriam per Dominum nostrum Jesum Christum.*[429]

Romanum on Good Friday).

[427] Marie-Benoît Schwalm, O.P., *Le Christ d'après Saint Thomas d'Aquin: Leçons, notes et commentaires recueillis et mis en ordre par le R. P. Menne O.P.* [Christ according to St. Thomas Aquinas: Readings, notes and commentaries, collected and arranged by Rev. Fr. Menne, O.P.] (Paris: Lethielleux, 1910), 256.

[428] Cf. Nicolaus Nilles, *De rationibus festorum sacratissimi cordis Jesu et purissimi cordis Mariae e fontibus juris canonici erutis* [On the reasons for the Feasts of the Sacred Heart of Jesus and the Immaculate Heart of Mary, drawn from the sources of canon law] (Oeniponte: Felizian Rauch, 1869; Nabu Press, 2011), 1:26, 87 and 167.

[429] "Thanks be to God, who hath given us the victory through our Lord Jesus Christ" (1Cor. 15:57).

Pro Aris et Focis [430]

Perhaps you ask me, and not without reason, how it is that some priests—educated, respected men, too—still refuse to bow before the majestic image of the Redeemer, who blesses those who believe in His love; how it is that they do not resolve to worship silently the daily triumphant procession of mercy....

But so it is. Old prejudices, the tendency to criticize everything, the itch to be considered learned and above all prejudices, a subtle self-satisfaction that wants to stand out *and call light darkness and darkness light;*[431] then too there may be lack of humility, a lack of interior life which, whatever the cost may be, is replaced by a vague religiosity without any precise notions or any depth; ... then perhaps the incursion of rationalism with an all-too-human view of Christianity; maybe also an old distaste for the supernatural, which awakens hidden pangs of conscience and brings to light an inner apostasy; maybe also the selfish answer to a devotion that demands works and not only words; maybe—why shouldn't we say so?—*circa fidem naufragaverunt.*[432] Very often, in my opinion, it is a mere question of attitude: an unconcealed sympathy for paradox; an innate tendency to deny known truth, to reject the historical evidence of the facts; the spirit of contradiction together with insufficient maturity of judgment. In this case it is useless to keep racking our brains: *neque si quis ex mortuis resurrexerit, credent.*[433]

Oh, if only all priests performed their duty in this regard by preaching everywhere the benefits, the beauties, the heavenly advantages of this godly devotion! Then the Heart of Jesus would soon be in fact the King of all Hearts, as He is by right.

The relatives and friends of the Divine Savior once said to Him, marveling at the sight of all His miraculous signs: *Si haec facis, manifesta teipsum mundo.*[434] We too, no doubt, clothe the same wish in different words; but do we reflect sufficiently on the fact that, of all people, we priests are the necessary instruments of this new epiphany, this *divine manifestation of the Sacred Heart of*

---

[430] For state and family.

[431] Isa. 5:20.

[432] "Some... have made shipwreck concerning the faith" (1 Tim. 1:19).

[433] "Neither will they believe, if one rise again from the dead" (Lk. 16:31).

[434] "If thou do these things, manifest thyself to the world" (Jn. 7:4).

Jesus? Did He not commission us to preach It to the people and to prepare the way for Him in souls? *Eritis mihi testes... usque ad ultimum terrae.*[435] The kingship of the Heart of Jesus in society will therefore be established above all by the deliberate, devoted work of the Catholic clergy.

How many times, O servant of God, do you repeat every day, perhaps distractedly, the sublime petitions of the Our Father! Reflect at least from time to time on these solemn words that the Church places on your lips, and know well: It is the will of God that His Name be hallowed, that His kingdom should come to us, *i.e.* that "we know His will and that we might reign with Him".[436]

If you really want this grace-filled kingdom, then without hesitation consecrate the children whom you have washed in the baptismal waters to the divine Heart; the youth who in their ardent imagination cling to golden dreams; married couples, whose union you bless, so that it will continue and be fruitful; sinners whose *clothes you wash in the Blood of the Lamb;*[437] the dying, whom you prepare for the final battle by the rite of anointing. And every morning, when you offer to the Heavenly Father the Heart of His only Son in the Host of peace—"the divine sacrifice of love, the most precious gift that you can offer"[438]—then lay one after the other all the souls for which you are responsible upon the most merciful bosom of Christ the Redeemer, this golden paten. Confidently implore Him for them: *ego pro eis rogo ..., quia tui sunt.*[439] And be assured that He saves them, because He wants to save them and can save them, because He has promised to do so and keeps His word, because He suffered so much for mankind and revealed to them His divine Heart, so as to convert them all to

[435] "You shall be witnesses unto me... even to the uttermost part of the earth" (Acts 1:8).

[436] Cf. St. Thomas Aquinas, *Summa Theologiae,* II-II, q. 83, art. 9, ad 4, where he clarifies the ideas of St. Augustine in *Epistola CXXX ad Probam, quomodo sit orandus Deus,* 11, 21; PL 33, 502.

[437] Cf. Apoc 7:14: "They... have washed their robes and have made them white in the blood of the Lamb."

[438] St. Margaret Mary, II, 519, 556, 591.

[439] "I pray for them... because they are thine" (Jn. 17:9).

His love: *Non est voluntas ante Patrem vestrum, ... ut pereat unus de pusillis istis.*[440] Pour then into these souls a blind, unlimited trust in the infinite love of Jesus, without fear, without hesitation, without discouragement, and believe—firmly believe that He "lets nothing perish that is consecrated to Him".[441] He is infinite goodness, He is overflowing redemption, He is God's forgiveness, He is the "eternal overseer of all resurrection".[442] *Salvare in perpetuum potest, accedentes per semetipsum ad Deum.*[443]

Above all, call to mind what I am about to tell you: *Haec meditare.*[444]

Despite the foolish objections of so many miserable "friends of humanity", despite the trivial curses of hundreds of hired demagogues, the best, most exquisite and most beneficial love consists today and always of bringing the heart of man closer to the Heart of God, so that God and man can be united in a sweet, everlasting embrace of love. Oh, when this devotion—an unfailing remedy for so many evils—takes possession of a soul, it turns it into the soul of a saint. If it makes its way into a family, it improves, purifies and transforms it. If it takes up residence in a religious community, one sees godliness flourish there very quickly. If it is spread to our villages, it soon transforms them into zealous homes

---

[440] "It is not the will of your Father who is in heaven, that one of these little ones should perish" (Mt. 18:14).

[441] St. Margaret Mary, II, 296, 300, 550.

[442] Caspar Cardinal Mermillod, Letter to the Bishop of Lüttich (3 September 1890).

[443] "He is able also to save forever them that come to God by him" (Heb. 7:25). Oh, how necessary trust in mercy is! Read the enchanting biography of Sr. Benigna Consolata, a Visitation nun from Como, a soul chosen by our Lord to be his "little secretary" and to preach His mercy to the world. You will find in it the magnificent words, noted by the divine teacher Himself, that open up hearts to a blind, limitless trust in the Sacred Heart of Jesus. Scatter these words all around you like seed, repeat them yourself to those who have fallen very far into error or vice! Tell them that a soul is that much closer to divine grace, the more it distant it thinks that it is from it, for nothing is more deserving of infinite mercy than a great spiritual need.

[444] "Meditate upon these things" (1 Tim. 4:15).

of Christian living, *quia non erit impossibile apud Deum omne verbum.*[445]

And the Heart of Jesus is able to triumph over these dubious political intrigues and over this *auri sacra fames,*[446] over these bitter fruits of education without God, over all these scandalous, challenging fashions, over these shameful marketplaces of human flesh, over this raging slaughter of souls, over these *deceits of false love,* which dry up the sources of life, over this miserable deterioration of science and art, over the complete secularization of welfare institutions, over the imprudent falsifications of the truth, over this ridiculous arrogance, over this despicable luxury and all other forms of contagious corruption; ... *ut sicut regnavit peccatum in mortem, ita et gratia regnet per justitiam, in vitam aeternam.*[447]

"If you believe," He is the one speaking here, "then you will see the power of My Heart in the splendor of My love."[448]

Per Mariam ad Jesum[449]

Servant of God, does the undertaking that the Church enjoins on you seem difficult? *Confortet te virtus Dei, Christus.*[450] Listen to the words that you find on the lips of the dying Redeemer: *Ecce mater tua!*[451] If you want to be a priest who really is holy and sanctifies others, then draw close to the Heart of Jesus *cum vero corde, in plenitudine fidei,*[452] so as to live by intimacy with His life; but never forget that He communicates this divine life through the hands of His Immaculate Mother, the treasurer of His divine Heart. For the great servants of this good Mother, who is *full of grace,*[453] is

---

[445] "Because no word shall be impossible with God" (Lk. 1:37).

[446] "Holy hunger for gold" [ironic, meaning "accursed hunger for gold"] (Virgil, Aeneid, Book III, verse 57).

[447] "That as sin hath reigned to death: so also grace might reign by justice unto life everlasting" (Rom. 5:21).

[448] St. Margaret Mary, II, 429.

[449] To Jesus through Mary.

[450] "Let Christ, the power of God, strengthen you" (St. Bernard of Clairvaux, *Sermo XX in Cantica Canticorum: De triplici modo dilectionis, quia Deum diligimus,* 4; PL 183, 868).

[451] "Behold thy mother" (Jn. 19:27).

[452] "With a true heart, in fulness of faith" (Heb. 10:22).

[453] Lk. 1:28. St. Thomas explained that Mary "is full of grace and the

reserved the priceless prerogative of living by Jesus Christ's fullness of life and communicating that life: *Sit in singulis Mariae anima, ut magnificet Dominum, sit in singulis spiritus Mariae, ut exultet in Deo.*[454] Therefore from now on turn to her with unbounded trust; may the thought of her never abandon you, may her gentle name be inscribed in your heart. Ask of her everything that you want for yourself and for souls; she is the Queen of Mercy, she is our life, our sweetness, our hope; she is the joy of every single priestly life.

Surrender yourself entirely into her hands by a perfect, irrevocable act of dedication, *et mutaberis in virum alium.*[455] You will see that you suddenly become purer, more zealous, more generous and more capable of understanding the knowledge of the saints. You will very suddenly see blossom in your soul the magnificent flower of devotion to the Divine Heart: *No one believed in love more than she!*[456]

It is a generally held principle among spiritual authors that the Most Blessed Virgin Mary is the mystical ladder to heaven: *per Mariam ad Jesum.* And in fact, when a prodigal son who through his sin has become a worker in a foreign land returns to our Lord through remorse; when a soul that has been astray for a long time finds truth and life again through a thousand storms, who prepared this return for that unfortunate soul if not she who by right is the *Queen of Hearts?* And does not the piety of the faithful invoke her under the sweet title of *Our Lady of the Sacred Heart of Jesus* so as to make us understand that we must necessarily go to Mary if we wish to reach Jesus safely, easily and quickly?

She is the blessed cause of our joy, the happy Mother of divine grace, the Queen and *Magistra* of the Sacred Heart of Jesus; in her

---

source of graces" on the basis of her divine maternity: *ita quod eum qui est plenus omni gratia, in se reciperet; et, eum pariendo, quodammodo gratiam ad omnes derivaret* ["so that she received within her Him Who is full of all grace; and by bringing Him forth, she, in a manner, dispensed grace to all"] (St. Thomas Aquinas, *Summa Theologiae*, III, q. 27, art. 5, ad 1).

[454] "Let Mary's soul be in individual [Christians], so as to glorify the Lord; let Mary's spirit be in them, so as to rejoice in God" (St. Ambrose, *Expositio Evangelii secundum Lucam* 1:44-45, II, 26; PL 15, 1561).

[455] "Thou ... shalt be changed into another man" (1 Kings 10:6).

[456] St. Francis de Sales proves this; cf. *Oeuvres de Saint François de Sales, Évêque et Prince de Genève et Docteur de l'Église* (Annecy: J. Niérat, 1892), 5:50-57; 4:191-195.

is all greatness, glory and splendor; in her is all joy and happiness, ... she is the "Paradise of the Incarnation":[457] *Nonne thesaurus Dei Maria? Ubicumque illa est, ibi et Cor ejus.*[458]

Per Mariam ad Jesum!

The visionary of Paray-le-Monial herself, the "victim of the Divine Heart,"[459] regarded the Blessed Virgin Mary as the normal way of reaching Jesus. "If a soul is a perfect daughter of Mary, then the Virgin makes her a true disciple of the Sacred Heart.... She will be a special protectress for this soul, so as to make it attain the life of perfection."[460] The saintly Visitation nun saw how the Sacred Heart of Jesus presented His sacrifice to His heavenly Father on the "altar of His Mother's heart".[461] No other ideal gladdened her short earthly existence so much as the thought of making the Heart of Jesus, "which lives in Mary's heart",[462] reign in all places.

Moreover, can we not declare with all theological precision that *the Heart of Jesus is the heart of Mary? Virga Maria, flos Mariae Christus*, St. Ambrose wrote.[463] A medieval author expresses our idea

---

[457] Title of a lecture by Fr. Jacques Marie Louis Monsabré: *L'exposition du Dogme catholique, conférence* 30. See also Dom Columba Marmion, O.S.B., *Christ, the Life of the Soul* (1917), chapter 12, "The Life of the Incarnate Word".

[458] "Is Mary not God's treasure? Wherever she is, there too is His heart" (St. Bernard of Clairvaux, *Sermones in festo Annuntiationis Beatae Mariae Virginis, Sermo III* [Lk 1:26-38], 7; PL 133, 396). Of course the saintly Doctor of the Church is not speaking about the Heart of Jesus but rather about the love of God, and yet the application to the Most Sacred Heart of Jesus is quite natural and justified (cf. Mt 6:21).

[459] St. Margaret Mary, II, 551.

[460] St. Margaret Mary, II, 558, 674.

[461] St. Margaret Mary, II, 750.

[462] St. Margaret Mary, II, 751. Meditate also on the beautiful prayer that the saint addresses to Our Lady (II, 781).

[463] "Mary is the stem, and Mary's blossom is Christ" (St. Ambrose, *Expositio Evangelii secundum Lucam,* 1:42-43, II, 24; PL 15, 1561). We are talking about the relationship between these Two Hearts, which for quite different reasons are the object of Catholic piety (see Terrien, *La dévotion au Sacré-Coeur,* Chapter 4; cf. footnote 26 of this book).

even more clearly when he says: *Caro enim Jesu, caro est Mariae.*[464]

Suppose for a moment, if you have the courage to do so, that the Blessed Virgin Mary had refused to pronounce her *fiat*—she was, after all, free. Would the Word of God have taken a human heart somewhere else? And if this shining star, this beneficial sun that gives life and warmth to souls, gladdens the firmament of the Church today, to whom else do we owe it than to the Virgin Mother *per quam meruimus auctorem vitae suscipere?*[465]

The Sacred Heart of Jesus willed to be formed out of her utterly pure blood, nourished by her virginal milk, warmed by her tender affection and to spend long months in the womb of the Immaculata as a living Host in a precious tabernacle, so as to be *the Child of her love.*[466] And after such a long, ardent communion, after the sweet outpourings of love in Bethlehem and the joyful familiarity of Nazareth, a terrible lance pierced the still trembling Heart of Her adored Son before the eyes of His Mother after she had suddenly become shrouded in horror and darkness on Mount Calvary. Is it any wonder, then, if the sweet perfume of this tender heart still anoints the whole person of the Blessed Virgin Mary today, after so many centuries? Oh, how close to the Sacred Heart of Jesus we feel at the feet of our good Mother!

The Apostolate Among the Clergy

Perhaps you, dear reader, were until quite recently hesitant, biased, not very zealous, *debilis in amore!*[467] Who knows? Maybe you were cold and indifferent toward the adorable Heart of the

---

[464] "For the Flesh of Jesus is Mary's flesh" (Pseudo-Augustine, *Sermo de Assumptione B.M.V.*, 5; PL 40:1145). Even if this sermon is not by St. Augustine, as many believed, it deserved to be mentioned along with the works of that saint (Jean-Baptiste Terrien, S.J., *La Mère de Dieu et des hommes d'après les Pères et la théologie* [The Mother of God and of men according to the Church Fathers and theology], 4 vols. [Paris: Lethielleux, 1900, 1902], 4:479).

[465] "Through whom we merited to receive the Author of life" (*Breviarium Romanum, Oratio de B.M.V.; Missale Romanum, In Circumcisione Domini* (Feast of the Circumcision of Our Lord), Octave of Christmas, Prayer).

[466] [Regnum] *filii dilectionis suae* (cf. Vulgate: Col. 1:13).

[467] "Weak in love" (Thomas à Kempis, *The Imitation of Christ*, Book III, chapter 5).

Redeemer.... How happy I would consider myself if my few poor words, *tamquam Deo exhortante per nos*,[468] helped to kindle in you a love for the living symbol of this Divine Love and to turn you from a cold, sluggish disciple into a staunch servant, an ardent defender and a magnanimous apostle! Know that this has always been my keenest wish, my only ambition, the great ideal of my poor life: to lead priests to the Sacred Heart of Jesus. "If you knew how beneficial it is to love the Heart of Jesus and to be loved by It!"[469] Is this not an anticipation of Paradise?

Do not investigate to find out who wrote these simple, artless lines; *non quaeras quis hoc dixerit, sed quid dicatur attende.*[470]

The author? Oh, he is only a handful of ashes, a lost atom in the midst of this bounty of created things, a poor nothing, the shadow of a dream and the echo of the divine word: *vox clamantis.*[471] Be sure, therefore, that with me and before me Jesus, the King of glory,[472] spoke to you through my impure lips. He, the chief author of this book, wishes you to persevere in this devotion, which He has taught you to appreciate as is fitting. And it is His ardent wish— *desiderio desideravi*[473]—that you too might make use of these poor lines to warm other priestly hearts at the sacred fire of His love: *Ego autem rogavi pro te, ut non deficiat fides tua, et tu aliquando conversus, confirma fratres tuos.*[474]

My mission is completed, I retire with the awareness of having carried out my precisely delineated task, of having obeyed a specific order: *Opus consummari quod dedisti mihi ut faciam;*[475] *vae enim mihi est, si non evangelizavero!*[476]

---

[468] "God as it were exhorting by us" (2Cor. 5:20).

[469] St. Margaret Mary, II, 345, 678.

[470] "Ask not who said this, but pay attention to what is said" (Thomas à Kempis, *The Imitation of Christ*, Book I, chapter 5).

[471] "The voice of one crying" (Jn. 1:23).

[472] 1Cor. 2:8.

[473] "With desire I have desired" (Lk. 22:15).

[474] "I have prayed for thee, that thy faith fail not: and thou, being once converted, confirm thy brethren" (Lk. 22:32).

[475] "I have finished the work which thou gavest me to do" (Jn. 17:4).

[476] "Woe is unto me if I preach not the gospel" (1Cor. 9:16).

And now I hand the weapons over to you, *ut milites in illis bonam militiam.*[477] Win for this kindly Heart new worshippers in spirit and in truth; awaken for It new apostles. Make use of all divine and human means, all the means of your vocation, all the talents that nature has given you along the way, all the gifts of grace; proclaim in a loud voice the rights of Divine Love; repeat to others what I have told you: *quod in aure auditis, praedicate super tecta.*[478]

May difficulty not discourage you, nor contradiction disarm you: *Sit etiam fortis et constans amor tuus, nec cedens terroribus, nec succumbens laboribus.*[479] Work with faith and persistence, without ever growing weary: *Argue, increpa,* but above all *obsecra*[480] by action, by example, with the pen, through prayer, through the tactful business that the love of Christ can inspire, and be assured that these efforts will produce consoling results: *scientes quod labor vester non est inanis in Domino.*[481] Let your activity be as well-planned as it is generous, *in omni patientia et doctrina;*[482] let it be calm, polite, prudent: *Nemo adolescentiam tuam contemnet.*[483] And then, forward, without fear! If you knew how precious the *holy crusade* for the Heart of Jesus is to the Lord, how blessed it is by heaven! God wills it!

Unfortunately you will also find servants of the sanctuary who smile at logic and the Gospel, *sanam doctrinam non sustinebunt, et*

---

[477] "That thou war in them a good warfare" (1 Tim. 1:18).

[478] "That which you hear in the ear, preach ye upon the house tops" (Mt. 10:27). The book by Fr. René Henry, C.Ss.R., *Pasce agnos meos: Le Prêtre héraut du Sacré-Coeur* [Feed my sheep: The Priest as the herald of the Sacred Heart] (Paris: Librairie Téqui, Imprimerie Saint-Paul, 1927), is very useful for the clergy, above all because of the practical suggestions of a pedagogical and pastoral nature that it contains concerning devotion to the Sacred Heart of Jesus.

[479] "May your love be strong and steadfast, not yielding to terrors nor overcome by toils" (St. Bernard of Clairvaux, *Sermo XX in Cantica Canticorum: De triplici modo dilectionis, qua Deum diligimus,* 4; PL 183, 869).

[480] "Reprove, entreat, ... rebuke" (2 Tim. 4:2).

[481] "Knowing that your labour is not in vain in the Lord" (1 Cor. 15:58).

[482] "In all patience and doctrine" (2 Tim. 4:2).

[483] "Let no man despise thy youth" (1 Tim. 4:12).

a veritate quidem auditum avertent.[484] So what? *Oportet et haereses esse*;[485] *necesse est enim ut veniant scandala.*[486] You, though, be an apostle to them, *opus fac evangelistae*;[487] "contradiction is one of the infallible signs that God is being glorified through the reign of the Sacred Heart of Jesus."[488]

And if it seems to you at first that you are achieving little, then do not be discouraged, but hope like Abraham *against all hope.*[489] "It is enough to make the Divine Heart known and then to leave it up to Him to imbue with the unction of His grace the hearts that He has chosen for Himself."[490] "This Heart will see to it that It is known and loved, even by those who oppose It."[491] Of course you must not neglect the simple faithful. But carry out your apostolate especially among the clergy. One priest outweighs a whole legion of laymen. Moreover the sanctification of a soul consecrated to God is the shortest path to improving a whole population and thus surely and effectively contributing to the sanctification of mankind and the renewal of all things in Christ.

You young servants of God, who with indomitable courage fight the Lord's holy battles and generously take upon yourselves *pondus diei et aestus*,[492] allow me to remind you—and this will be for you the utmost consolation in your bitterness—that the protection of heaven is sure for all those who fight under the banner of the Heart of Jesus, *ut tempus hujus vitae... transeant cum victoria, per Christi virtutem.*[493]

---

[484] "They will not endure sound doctrine but... will indeed turn away their hearing from the truth" (2Tim. 4:3-4).

[485] "There must be also heresies" (1Cor. 11:19).

[486] "It must needs be that scandals come" (Mt. 18:7).

[487] "Do the work of an evangelist" (2Tim. 4:5).

[488] St. Margaret Mary, II, 356.

[489] Rom. 4:18.

[490] St. Margaret Mary, II, 490.

[491] St. Margaret Mary, II, 478.

[492] "Have borne the burden of the day and the heat" (Mt. 20:12).

[493] "So that they might pass through the time of this life victoriously through Christ's power" (St. Thomas Aquinas, *Super Evangelium Matthaei*, 4, 1, on Mt. 4:1-11).

The dear Saint, who has so often guided us and taught us trust with incomparable authority, wrote: "All who spend themselves for the salvation of souls ... will work with miraculous results... if they are imbued with a tender devotion to the Sacred Heart of Jesus."[494] Let us therefore direct souls to this divine lighthouse, and let us support in them, through a serious, well-organized apostolate, a tender confidence in the abyss of the mercy of Jesus Christ: let us help Him with a calm firmness in our convictions, with all the verve of our youthful zeal, *corde magno et animo volenti*[495] to carry out His plan of love. *Omnia traham ad meipsum.*[496]

Ante Tribunal Christi[497]

Oh, the decisive moment will come for us too, and certainly soon: the cut-off point between time, which is fleeting, and eternity, the only thing that lasts. *Quae est enim vita vestra? Vapor est ad modicum parens.*[498]

The harvest is abundant and the laborers are few; it is not surprising, therefore, when the good worker one day sinks down onto the laboriously tilled earth! *Nisi granum frumenti... mortuum fuerit, ipsum solum manet.*[499] But it is a work of justice for the weeds to be separated once and for all from the wheat, and for every unfruitful tree that our heavenly Father did not plant to be rooted up.[500] This is the mission entrusted to the angels of the Lord: *Colligent de regno ejus omnia scandala.*[501]

My God, how sad the lot of those priests must be who have never loved the Heart of Jesus in earnest, who have presumed—

.

---

[494] St. Margaret Mary, II, 628.

[495] "With a great heart and a willing mind" (2Mach. 1:3).

[496] "I ... will draw all things to myself" (Jn. 12:32).

[497] Before the judgment seat of Christ.

[498] "For what is your life? It is a vapour which appeareth for a little while" (Jas. 4:15).

[499] "Unless the grain of wheat... die, itself remaineth alone" (Jn. 12:24-25)

[500] Cf. Mt. 15:13.

[501] "They shall gather out of his kingdom all scandals and them that work iniquity" (Mt. 13:41).

mysterium iniquitatis![502]—to judge His words, to critique His promises and revelations, in their shortsightedness to condemn His infinite mercy, who responded to His thirst for love with contempt or reprehensible carelessness! *Non noverunt Patrem, neque me.*[503]

"The entrance to His Sacred Heart will be shut against them, because they drove Him out of theirs."[504] And what will become of these unfortunate souls? *Horrendum est incidere in manus Dei viventis!* [505]

Unfortunate anointed of the Lord, who have misused their authority and with their insidious hair-splitting, ridiculous subtleties and bold, deceptive arguments, with their knowledge that St. Paul denounced as *falsely so-called,*[506] by the example of their careless, unruly lives, have driven souls away from this merciful, kindly Heart in which "they might have found all graces by which to snatch them from the abyss of perdition."[507] Let us listen to Jesus' words: "[Woe to him] that shall scandalize one of these little ones that believe in me!"[508] And once again He is the one who utters this complaint: "Shed tears of sorrow over the callousness of these hearts that I have elected so as to consecrate them to My love."[509]

Unhappy priests, *falsi testes Dei.*[510] One is horrified to think of their first meeting with the divine Savior, who has now become their implacable Judge! *Qui spernit me et non accepit verba mea, habet qui judicet eum!*[511] With what might and with what anger in His voice will he say to each one of them: *Ego sum Jesus quem tu persequeris!*[512] And how stern their judgment will be! *Osculum*

---

[502] "The mystery of iniquity" (2 Thess. 2:7).

[503] "They have not known the Father nor me" (Jn. 16:3).

[504] St. Margaret Mary, II, 373.

[505] "It is a fearful thing to fall into the hands of the living God" (Heb. 10:31).

[506] 1 Tim. 6:20.

[507] St. Margaret Mary, II, 70.

[508] Mt. 18:6.

[509] St. Margaret Mary, II, 181, 182.

[510] "False witnesses of God" (1 Cor. 15:15).

[511] "He that despiseth me and receiveth not my words hath one that judgeth him" (Jn. 12:48).

[512] "I am Jesus whom thou persecutest" (Acts 9:5).

mihi non dedisti! ... Oleo caput meum non unxisti![513] *Quoties volui congregare filios tuos... et noluisti!*[514] How terribly severe will the revenge of spurned love make itself felt against them! *Et tunc confitebor illis, quia nunquam novi vos.*[515]

Venite, Benedicti[516]

In contrast, Jesus will console, *tanquam si nutrix foveat filios suos,*[517] the good priests who honored and preached this sweet symbol of Divine Love and defended it against the attacks of the godless and the foolish; these priests who are consecrated and offered up to Him, who have been transformed by Him, *in quo tota spes salvandorum consistit et meritum.*[518] In that decisive moment He will be their refuge, they will not die in His disfavor,[519] and "their names", which for many years already "have been enlisted in the Sacred Heart of Jesus will never be struck from It,"[520] for "He will eternally remember what they did for His honor."[521] And did Margaret Mary not write also that "He will take care of us and, despite all the storms, will bring us to the harbor of salvation, if we are consecrated and devoted to this adorable Heart"?[522]

One *little saint* said in her candid simplicity that "in the evening of our life we will be judged by our love,"[523] and certainly you have

---

[513] "Thou gavest me no kiss.... My head with oil thou didst not anoint" (Lk. 7:45-46).

[514] "How often would I have gathered together they children ... and thou wouldst not?" (Mt. 23:37).

[515] "And then I will profess unto them: I never knew you" (Mt. 7:23).

[516] "Come, ye blessed" (Mt. 25:34)

[517] "As if a nurse should cherish her children" (1 Thess. 2:7).

[518] "In Whom consists all the hope and merit of those that shall be saved" (Thomas à Kempis, *The Imitation of Christ*, Book IV, chapter 1).

[519] St. Margaret Mary, II, 397.

[520] St. Margaret Mary, II, 303.

[521] St. Margaret Mary, II, 408.

[522] St. Margaret Mary, II, 291.

[523] St. Thérèse of the Child Jesus. [Editor's note: This passage cannot be found in the writings of St. Thérèse; it is a quotation from the letters of St. John of the Cross.]

not forgotten this saying from the Gospel: *Many sins are forgiven her, because she hath loved much.*[524]

How much fear and how much useless sadness will burden our final agony, when after a long, busy priestly ministry we try to look at our actions, one after the other, in the light of eternity! *Qui invenietur ita immunis a culpa, ut in eo non habeat vel justitia quod arguat, vel misericordia quod remittat?*[525]

Maybe we were not always *lucerna ardens et lucens.*[526] Maybe occasionally "vanity" and "lying"[527] fought for possession of our poor heart, and the deceptive attraction of creatures—*fascinatio nugacitatis*[528]—all too often diminished the zeal of our heart.... Maybe for a moment we dragged the chaste garment of Jesus Christ through the mud....

How small and poor we will seem to ourselves in the grand solemnity of our last moment! We will then have to regard ourselves as useless servants! We will stand there with empty hands! ...

But no, my confreres, "the Holy Ghost still keeps the Heart of Jesus open for mercy and allows us to find in this adorable Savior an Advocate who ceaselessly makes intercession on our behalf."[529] Why then should we worry about it? Why should we live in fear and anxiety? *Neque mors, neque vita ... poterit nos separare a caritate Dei, quae est in Christo Jesu.*[530]

---

[524] Lk. 7:47.

[525] "Who shall be found so sinless that justice will have nothing to accuse him of and mercy nothing to forgive?" (St. Leo the Great, *Sermo XXXVII: In Epiphaniae solemnitate VII,* 3; PL 54, 258).

[526] "A burning and a shining light" (Jn. 5:35).

[527] Ps. 4:3.

[528] "The bewitching of vanity" (Wis. 4:12).

[529] André-Marie Meynard, *Traité de la vie intérieure, ou petite somme de théologie ascétique et mystique, d'après l'esprit et les principes de Saint Thomas d'Aquin* [Treatise on the interior life, or a little summa of ascetical and mystical theology, according to the mind and principles of St. Thomas Aquinas] (Paris: P. Lethielleux, 1929, 1949), Part I, chapter 1.

[530] "Neither death nor life ... shall be able to separate us from the love of God which is in Christ Jesus" (Rom. 8:38-39).

See around your bed of pain the rich crown of souls that you have won through your sacrifices and tears for the Heart of the Master: *Modicae fidei, quare dubitasti?*[531] Tell him in all gratitude: *Verba quae dedisti mihi dedi eis... et crediderunt.... Ego te clarificavi super terram.*[532]

See, legions of angels are descending..., the long-awaited hour of reward has begun. And while heaven invites you to the feast, the holy Viaticum brings you the final kiss of the Sacred Heart of Jesus as a pledge and foretaste of endless inebriation: *Sepisum dabit, quia seipsum dedit.*[533]

O good and faithful servant, leave this life without regrets.... "Blessed are you who have believed. Now all those things shall be accomplished for you that were promised to you by the Lord."[534]

Listen one last time, you priests all over the world, to the confidante of Jesus Christ, who encourages you for your great journey: "How beautiful it is to die, if one has had a tender, constant devotion to the Heart of Him who will be our Judge!"[535]

Sacred Heart of Jesus, I place my trust in Thee!

---

[531] "O thou of little faith, why didst thou doubt?" (Mt. 14:31).

[532] "The words which thou gavest me, I have given to them... and they have believed.... I have glorified thee on the earth" (Jn. 17:8, 4).

[533] "He will give Himself, because He gave Himself" (St. Augustine, Enarrationes in Psalmos XLII: Sermo ad populum: *In die jejunii, post meridiem habitus,* 2; PL 36, 477).

[534] Cf. Lk. 1:45.

[535] St. Margaret Mary, I, 275; II, 628.

Appendix One

Promises of Our Lord Jesus Christ to St. Margaret Mary Alacoque for Those who Honor His Divine Heart

The blessed Saint of Paray-le-Monial wrote one day that "the Sacred Heart of Jesus is worth ten million times more than His gifts."[536] We cannot doubt this truth. Yet it is also true that the promises of the Sacred Heart, collected and published by St. Margaret Mary, wonderfully incite souls to practice this salutary devotion quickly and generously.

In leaflets and devotional books we often find an inexact list of the promises of the Sacred Heart of Jesus, in which words of Our Lord are attributed to the Saint and words of the Saint are attributed to the Lord. As if this were not enough to create regrettable confusion, we find the words of our Lord and of St. Margaret Mary summarized, changed or unscrupulously adorned with commentary in ways that change the order and the meaning to suit the editor's taste. Moreover this list generally avoids citing sources and verifying the references to incompetent or negligent authors. Therefore I thought I would do priests a favor if I presented to them an *exact* text of the *Codex of Mercy,* which because of the duties of their state they should know, study, treasure and preach as the *Gospel of the Heart of Jesus.*

Two considerations of the Saint compelled me to recommend to servants of the Divine Heart careful, zealous study, pious meditation, and tireless propaganda of the promises. She said that "the treasures of blessing and grace contained in the Sacred Heart

---

[536] II, 552; cf. II, 253, 405.

of Jesus are infinite,"[537] and "The Heart of Jesus will reign, despite Satan and all who try to oppose Him."[538]

Furthermore it is necessary to consider that this great variety of promises, of greater or lesser importance, varying in their scope and extent, are found scattered in astonishing abundance in all of Margaret Mary's writings. They are often repeated, while sometimes they elaborate and clarify one another. The twelve summarized promises were recorded as an excerpt from the main groups that I have arranged here (we do not know who did it or when), and the Church approved them, although they do not really reproduce the thoughts and expressions of the saintly seer of Paray, except *ad sensum.*[539]

As for the dogmatic value of private revelations which the Church has approved (our Saint had approximately seventy of them), and whether Catholics are obliged in faith to accept them, I refer the reader to Johann Baptist Cardinal Franzelin, S.J., *De Divina traditione et scriptura* (1882), 282; Benedict XIV, *Opus de servorum Dei beatificatione et Beatorum canonisatione,* 4 vols. (1734-1738), II, chap. 32; Ioannis Cardinal De Lugo, S.J., *Disputationes scholasticae et morales,* Vol. I, *De virtute fidei Divinae* [1645] (Paris, 1868), Disputation 1, no. 228; easier to read and clearer is Jean Vincent Bainvel, *Devotion to the Sacred Heart: The Doctrine and Its History* (London: Burns Oates and Washbourne, 1926), Part 1, Chap. 4, §2. As for its historical value, see Auguste Hamon, S.J., *Histoire de la dévotion au Sacré-Coeur* [History of Devotion to the Sacred Heart], 5 vols., (Paris: Gabriel Beauchesne, 1923-1940), Vol. I, Chap. 6, p. 183.

---

[537] II, 627.

[538] II, 489; cf. II, 465, 354, 402, 429, 436, 537, 548, 614, 105 and other passages. I list so many references to prove that this very comforting statement recurs on the inspired lips of the saintly nun like a refrain, so as to rule out the possibility of assuming that it was only a lofty or insignificant expression.

[539] "With respect to their meaning." I carefully compiled all the sentences of St. Margaret Mary that have the character of a promise, although they sometimes are not presented directly in such expressions. But since I am addressing the clergy of the whole world, I have left out several promises that have a less general character, such as those pertaining to the King of France and the French nation, the Jesuit Order or the Visitation Order.

I. For Those who Work for the Salvation of Souls

"My Divine Redeemer informed me that those who work for the salvation of souls have the gift touching even the hardest hearts; if only they themselves cultivate a tender devotion to the Divine Heart, they will work with marvelous success, ... if they work to commend this devotion and to spread it everywhere, ... and if they draw all their light from this source."[540]

"It is enough to make the Divine Heart known and then to leave it up to Him to imbue with the unction of His grace the hearts (that He has chosen for Himself)."[541]

"The most hardened hearts ... and the souls most burdened by sin will be led by this means to salutary repentance."[542]

"There is nothing gentler, nothing milder and at the same time nothing stronger or more effective than the gentle unction of the burning love of this lovable Heart in order to convert the most hardened souls and to penetrate the most callous hearts by the words of His preachers and true friends, whom he makes like a flaming sword that causes frozen hearts to melt in His love."[543]

II. For Those who Want to be Better

"I hope that this Divine Heart will become an overflowing, inexhaustible source of mercy[544] and grace..., to appease God's righteous anger over so many sins," and God will "forgive sinners in view of the love that He has for this Sacred Heart." The Sacred Heart of Jesus is "like a fortress and a sure refuge for all poor sinners who want to flee to it to escape Divine Justice."[545]

---

[540] II, 439, 407, 628.

[541] II, 490.

[542] II, 536.

[543] II, 557.

[544] The popularized text of the promises speaks about an "ocean of mercy"; this statement is nowhere to be found in the Saint's writings. She uses the expression "ocean of the Sacred Heart of Jesus" (II, 405), without specifying further. We know that St. Catharine of Siena calls God an "ocean of peace."

[545] II, 363, 429.

"The Sacred Heart of Jesus is all-powerful... to obtain mercy."[546]

"The most effective means we have available to rise up from our fall is the Sacred Heart of Our Lord Jesus Christ."[547]

"The Sacred Heart of Jesus wants to restore life to many through this means, by drawing them back from the paths of destruction and destroying Satan's reign in souls, so as to establish in them the reign of love."[548]

"I know of no other pious exercise in the spiritual life better suited to lead a soul to the highest degree of perfection in a short time."[549]

III. For Souls of Good Will

"Persons living in the world find by means of this loving devotion all the helps they need in their state of life."[550]

The Sacred Heart of Jesus "will give peace to families,[551] reunite broken families[552] and assist and protect those that are in any need."[553]

"He will support them in their works,[554] consol them in their troubles,[555] and bless all their endeavors."[556]

"Persons who devote themselves to this Heart will find in it a place of refuge during their lifetime and especially at the hour of their death."[557]

"Evidently there is no one in this world who will not receive all sorts of help from heaven, provided that he has a truly grateful love for Jesus Christ, such as is shown Him by devotion to His Sacred Heart."[558]

---

[546] II, 300.
[547] II, 159.
[548] II, 437, 363, 489, 550, 571.
[549] II, 627.
[550] II, 627.
[551] II, 627.
[552] II, 296, 300.
[553] II, 296, 300.
[554] II, 628.
[555] II, 628.
[556] II, 628.
[557] II, 628, 550.
[558] II, 628.

"Those who practice this devotion to the Sacred Heart will never perish,"[559] for "a child never perishes in the arms of an Almighty Father."[560]

"Oh, how good it is to die if one has a tender, constant devotion to the Heart of Him who is our Judge!"[561]

"Ah, if I were only allowed to make public the infinite riches that are hidden in this precious treasure (*i.e.* the Sacred Heart of Jesus) and with which He enriches His true friends."[562]

"If only I could tell all that I know about this lovable devotion and could reveal to the whole world the treasures of grace that Jesus Christ keeps contained in this adorable Heart and that He would like to pour out abundantly upon all who practice this devotion!"[563]

"His love compels Him to pour out the inexhaustible treasure of His sanctifying, healing graces on souls of good will."[564]

IV. For all who Consecrate Themselves to the Heart of Jesus

"If you knew how much merit and glory there is in honoring this lovable Heart, ... and what the reward is for those who strive only for this honor after consecrating themselves to Him!"[565]

"If we have consecrated ourselves to this adorable Heart, ... then it will take care of us and bring us to the harbor of salvation despite the storms."[566]

"Anyone who gives himself completely to God by consecrating himself to the Heart of Jesus ... makes his salvation sure."[567]

"I cannot believe that persons consecrated to the Heart of Jesus will perish, nor that they will fall under Satan's dominion through mortal sin, ... if they conform in everything to His holy teachings."[568]

---

559 II, 328, 528, 345, 550.

560 II, 386, 411.

561 II, 628.

562 II, 533.

563 II, 626, 550.

564 II, 532.

565 II, 279.

566 II, 291.

567 II, 298.

568 II, 328.

"It seems to me that there is no surer means of salvation that to be consecrated to this Divine Heart.... None of those who are especially devoted and consecrated to this Heart will perish."[569]

V. For Apostles of the Sacred Heart of Jesus

Jesus "let me see that more names are inscribed (in His Heart) on account of their desire to further His honor; therefore He will never allow them to be blotted out."[570]

"He revealed to me treasures of love and graces for persons who consecrate themselves and sacrifice themselves to Him, so as to give Him all the honor, love and glory whatsoever that is in their power."[571]

"He will never allow them (the apostles of the Heart of Jesus) to perish and will be for them a safe refuge against all the attacks of their enemies, but above all at the hour of death; this Divine Heart will receive them with love, assure their salvation, take care to sanctify them and magnify them in the sight of His heavenly Father, to the extent that they strive to extend the reign of His love in hearts."[572]

"He promised to reward all the good that we do for Him with the treasures of His divine Heart."[573]

VI. For Religious Orders

"He promised me... to pour out the sweet anointings of His burning love upon all communities in which this divine image is honored and which place themselves under His special protection. He will turn aside the chastisements of divine justice so as to make them zealous again, if they have become lukewarm."[574] "He will keep all hearts united, so as to make them one with Him."[575]

---

[569] Cf. II, 344, 345; II, 346, 396, 437, 530, 585.

[570] II, 303, 408; the latter passage reads: "written in gold letters", so as to express the value and the merit of showing honor to the Heart of Jesus (cf. II, 109).

[571] II, 396.

[572] II, 532.

[573] II, 541.

[574] II, 296, 300, 532.

[575] II, 533.

"No other means is necessary in order to restore in the less edifying religious orders their initial zeal and the most exact observance of the Rule and to lead those who observe the Rule exactly to the highest degree of perfection."[576]

"How many blessings and graces ... has He resolved to pour out on the communities that offer Him the most honor and glory!"[577]

VII. For Homes in Which His Image is Revered

"He promised me that He will abundantly pour out all the treasures of grace with which He Himself is filled on the hearts of all who revere it *(i.e.* the image of the Heart of Jesus); wherever this image is displayed for particular honor, it will call down all sorts of blessings."[578]

"Since He is the source of all blessings, He will pour them out abundantly upon all places where this image of His lovable Heart is displayed to be loved and honored."[579]

VIII. For Those who Celebrate the Feast of the Heart of Jesus

"I ask you that the first Friday after the Octave of Corpus Christi be dedicated to a special feast to honor My Heart.... I promise you, that My Heart will expand so as to pour out abundantly the influence of its divine love on those who pay it this honor and work to promote it."[580]

"The day of this feast is a day of salvation and eternal blessing for all who celebrate it with honor, with a humble, sincere heart."[581]

---

[576] II, 627.

[577] II, 431.

[578] I, 244.

[579] II, 296, 300, 532.

[580] II, 103. The promise concerns first all who institute the feast and then those who celebrate it.

[581] II, 444, 439.

IX. For The Practice of the "Nine First Fridays"

"In the abundance of the mercy of My Heart I promise the grace of final perseverance to all those who, during nine consecutive months, will receive Holy Communion on the first Friday of every month; they will not die in My disgrace, but will receive the Sacraments, and My Heart will be a sure shelter for them in their final hour."[582]

♥

This promise is historically beyond doubt, just like the others, for until 1792 the handwritten text was preserved by the Visitation Nuns in Dijon;[583] moreover it offers the utmost guarantee of authenticity, because it alone was specially examined and approved by the Congregation for Sacred Rites.[584] There are discrepancies in many commentaries on this promise, and (what is even stranger) there was a genuine conspiracy of silence about it. Thus it remained hidden and unknown to the Christian people until 1869, when Father de Franciosi publicized it.

Were they afraid that it was theologically untenable? Or that the faithful would misuse it? That it would provide an excuse for non-Catholics to mock? All these questions were answered convincingly by worthy authors.[585]

---

[582] These words are found in Letter 86 to Monsieur de Saumaise (II, 397) and in *The Life*, written by the Saint's contemporaries (I, 261) in approximately the same words. To decide which version is preferable, see Auguste Hamon, S.J., "*Le texte de 'La grande promesse du Coeur'*" [The text of 'The Great Promise of the Sacred Heart'], in: *Études [publiées par de Pères de la Compagnie de Jésus, Paris]* 40/95 (20 June 1903): 854-857 and idem, *Histoire de la dévotion au Sacré-Coeur,* vol. I, chap. 13.

[583] Hamon, *ibid.*; Miguel Garcia Estébanez, S.J., *La grande promesse du Coeur de Jésus: étude historique, théologique et pratique* (Paris: Gabriel Beauchesne, 1913), 10.

[584] Jean-Baptiste Terrien, S.J., *La dévotion au Sacré-Coeur de Jésus, d'après les documents authentiques et la théologie* (Paris: Lethielleux), II and Appendix 4; Estébanez, op. cit., 18.

[585] See Xavier-Marie Le Bachelet, "*La grande promesse du Sacré Coeur*", in: *Études* 38/88 (August 1901): 385-394 at 385; Arthur Vermeersch, S.J.,

Certainly it is no longer permissible to doubt the authenticity of the document; and so too "theologians have the right ... to draw all the conclusions that are not inconsistent with sacred science."[586]

Incidentally, the promised grace is not new to the Church; in its basic outline it is consistent with the privilege of the *Scapular of Mount Carmel.*[587]

Final perseverance, *i.e.* dying in a state of grace, is granted under this *conditio sine qua non* [indispensable condition]: *The reception of Holy Communion on nine consecutive First Fridays of the month.* These words are clear and make the effectiveness of receiving communion on the first Sunday, instead of the First Friday, doubtful at least. We may also conclude that any interruption in the series, even involuntarily, means the loss of any right to this privilege.

These Communions must be received with the intention of honoring the Sacred Heart of Jesus and participating in the promised effect. Nevertheless it is enough to make this intention once explicitly at the beginning of the practice, without revoking it, in other words, to have the intention virtually. It is not necessary to actualize this intention each time, *i.e.* to renew it on all nine First Fridays.

Of course these must be *worthy* Communions, *i.e.* received in a state of grace; yet to achieve this requires no special zeal that

---

Pratique et Doctrine de la Dévotion au Sacré-Coeur de Jésus, 2 vols. (Paris, Tournai: Casterman), vol. 2; Henri Ramière, S.J., *Mois du Sacré-Coeur 33e jour* [Month of the Sacred Heart, Day 33].

[586] Hamon, *"Le texte de 'La grande promesse du Coeur'"*, in *Études* 40/95 (20 June 1903): 857. As for the classic objection that tries to destroy the authority of the great promise at its root, see *Oportet illum regnare* [He must rule], 2nd edition, p. 344.

[587] Concerning the historical value of the privilege that was granted to St. Simon Stock, read the book edited by Benedictus Zimmerman, *Monumenta historica Carmelitana* (Lérins: Ex typis Abbatiae, 1907), which was approved by the Superiors of the Order, and also the interesting article by the theologian Emilio Campana (1874-1939, from Lugano) in the April 1923 issue of the periodical *Regina dei Cuori* [Queen of Hearts]. Obviously it would be very unwise to preach the conclusions of the aforementioned article. However insightful and justified they are, they would nevertheless be *piarum aurium offensivae* [offensive to pious ears].

would be entirely beyond the capability of many persons.[588] The efficacy is promised to the series of prescribed Communions, but is not dependent on the zeal, the sacrifices and the acts of virtue that may accompany them.

All may believe with *moral certainty* that they will be saved if they *more humano* [according to the rules of human action] have fulfilled the conditions required by the Sacred Heart of Jesus, and that they will be saved through the *fact* that they really have fulfilled them.[589]

Even serious sins committed between two Communions do not revoke the privilege, provided that they are properly confessed before the next Communion; even someone who after completing the series of nine Holy Communions happens to fall into mortal sin does not have to consider himself excluded from the promised favor that he has already obtained. He may confess and have trust in God's almighty love.

Sinlessness is not promised, but only *death in the state of God's grace* and the salvation of the soul, even though it may be *per ignem* [as though through fire]. This privilege in fact does not rule out a more or less long stay in Purgatory. As for the Sacraments of Penance and Extreme Unction, we can be sure of receiving both— at least Extreme Unction—*only in the case* where they would be necessary in order to put the soul into the state of grace. If a dying person who has received the nine Communions is in the state of God's grace, then it may very well happen that he will die without the sacraments, because they are not necessary to save him. The promise nevertheless has its main effect, which is to open to him the gates of Paradise.

Of course it is an excellent thing to repeat the series of required Communions *several times,* so as to be that much more certain of

---

[588] The contrary opinion was advanced by Fr. Franciscus Adolphus Ludovicus Smit, S.J., (among others) in Maandrozen (the Dutch *Messenger of the Sacred Heart of Jesus*).

[589] See Arthur Vermeersch, S.J., "*La grande promesse du Sacré Coeur*", in Études 40/95 (5 June 1903): 593-600 at 593. Father Santos Bengoechea, S.J., in his short work *Pignora aeternae praedestinationis* [Pledges of eternal predestination] makes numerous exceptions. This is a "moral certainty that is sufficient to dispel any anxiety, without however making room for any arrogant presumption" (cf. Vermeersch, "*La grande promesse*", *ibid.,* 599).

the outcome. The fact is that we can never be metaphysically sure that we have received the Communions in a state of grace.

For us priests who celebrate Holy Mass every day, it is enough to make the resolution to celebrate *all First Fridays* of the month during our whole life for the intention of meriting the effect of the promise. When one series of Masses is ended, we begin with the next, without it being necessary to renew the intention.[590]

Given the uncertainty of salvation that was proclaimed by the Council of Trent—and even after the proclamation of the promise, this dogma remains dreadfully true—it is easy to see the importance of this special privilege in calming the anxieties and fears of all who have been impressed by the all-too-painful experience of their own wickedness or weakness.

"The cause is entirely disproportionate to the effect!" some will say. That is true, but are we forgetting that between the effect and the cause there is *infinite mercy?*

❤

Oh how good it would be if God's servants would often renew their courage and strengthen their hopes, which often grow unsure and weak in dealing with hard, difficult reality, and would do so through meditation, or even better through the silent, intimate contemplation of this *Codex of Love,* which was drawn up in keeping with perfect divine criteria, *ubi abundavit delictum, superabundavit gratia.*[591]

On the other hand, who could express in words the bitterness that we feel when we reflect that more than just one priest has never been willing to celebrate the nine Masses demanded by the Lord, nor to require his penitents to make the nine First Fridays!

Is it faith that is lacking? Is it love? ...

Maybe both.

---

[590] Sometimes it happens that the First Friday of the month of April falls on Good Friday, a "non-liturgical" day; in this case the series is interrupted, at least probably. It would be wise to begin over in this case.

[591] "Where sin abounded, grace did more abound" (Rom. 5:20).

Appendix Two

Message of the Heart of Jesus to the heart of priests[592]

I am cold! I am thirsty! I am hungry.... Tell my good priests, so that they may warm Me with their love, that they may give Me souls, souls, souls.... Did I not die for love of souls?

All the treasures of My Heart lie open.

The more the nations stray from Me and reject Me, the more My sweet Mother urges Me to open up the treasures of love, mercy and sanctification that My Heart contains.

Certainly, devotion to My Heart is very widespread; it gives Me consolation and leads a lot of souls to Me, the Savior of souls. And yet *people are still far from understanding the infinite treasures of My Heart!* ... My Mother asks Me, My Heart urges Me to pour out these treasures and to invite good souls to sink into this sea of mercy and to lose themselves in it....

Take this appeal of My Heart to the ends of the earth, bring it especially to My priest, who is to dear to Me! My priest, My

---

[592] This exhortation was found by the Marist missionary Father Le Cerf among the spiritual writings left by his confrere, Father Nicolet, who was a seminary rector and died in Rome in March 1900. The handwriting was not that of the deceased Marist, and everything points to the fact that he had received this document from a blessed soul, because the message that it contains really seems to flow from the Heart of our Lord Himself.

With the approval of Pope St. Pius X it was circulated throughout the world and did much good for many priests.

Read it from time to time, O Elect of the Divine Heart; meditate on the words, make them the object of your examination of conscience. This message will do you good, too.

alter ego, My "second self"! ... If they would only understand My yearning desire to be most intimately united *with each and every one of them!* ... Rare are those who attain this perfect union that My Heart has prepared for them on earth.... And what is needed to attain it?

One must gather all the inclinations of love, in a certain sense unite them and direct them to Me, who abide in the innermost depths of your soul. Ah, proclaim it to all who toil for Me in the icy terrain of the North, to those who languish in the torrid South, the brave heroes who fight under My banner, to those who consume themselves day and night in ministering to souls, who have their fill of persecutions, labors and contradictions in My service. To all of them *proclaim how much I love them, implore them to hear this loving, urgent appeal of My Heart,* my tender invitation to descend into the depths of their soul, so as to unite themselves there with Me, who never leave them, and in a sense to become one with Me.... With how many blessings will I then enrich them!

This mysterious, divine union will be the beginning of a much holier and more fruitful life than they have led until now....

Many priests know very well the doctrine of the union of the soul with Me, several strive for it; but how few, even among pious, zealous priests, even among My most devoted friends, know that *I am there, in the depths of their soul,* and burn with the desire to make them one with Me....

And why? Because they live on the surface of their soul. Ah, if they would tear themselves aware from external things and human impressions, so as to descend *alone into the innermost recess of their soul, to the very depths, to the place where I am*; how soon they would find Me, and what a life of union, of light and love would then be theirs....

Many, many priests who are on the right path and exercise a certain vigilance over themselves are content with that and seek no further.... They should only go, full of trust, to My Mother, who is also their Mother. How she loves them, My priests, how she appeals to Me for them! And once again: She, My sweet Mother, is the one who urges Me to make all the treasures of My Heart accessible and to send out a new appeal to all good souls, especially to My dear priests.

She, My tender Mother, is the delight of My Heart; may she be your delight also! For know that this Mother of Divine Love possesses the secret of this marvelous union that My Heart now offers to all its priests as a new, extraordinary means of sanctification through an immeasurable outpouring of mercy and love.

Appendix Three

Blessed Eduard Poppe: Enthronement of the Sacred Heart of Jesus in my Priestly cell

O my dear Jesus, my God, my Redeemer and my perfect model, welcome to my modest priestly cell. I adore you with my whole being and acknowledge You as my supreme King. I give You the place of honor in my cell, whereby I mean to tell you that I regard You as the Teacher, the Lord and leader of my whole priestly life. I bring You here, O my divine Friend, so as to dwell with You here, to work with You here, and to live with you here. I have reserved for You a place in my cell, very close to me, because I would like to be more intimately united with You, so as to think, arrange my life and work more and more according to Your mind and Your view of things.... Lord Jesus, my King and my Friend, how much I need You! I love You so little from the depths of my soul, I so easily lose sight of You, I speak so little with You. I work with such a deficient supernatural intention, with so much vanity and with merely human busyness; my work produces so little fruit. O my King of love, infinitely affectionate Lover of souls, You have chosen me to go and bear fruit, fruit that will last. This is my most ardent desire too. Souls, all the time souls!

This is why I have prepared for You hear a dwelling place and a throne. I would like to begin a new life with You: a life of love, a fruitful life.

I will sit down at my desk with Your picture before my eyes, in Your sight. I will never set foot in my cell and never leave it without kneeling down and asking for Your blessing. Before I reach for my pen, before I open a book, I will look at You, with my hand on my heart, to ask You for help and advice. Before I open a letter or write one, I will lift up my eyes to You, to obtain light and blessing. During my spiritual reading, while studying, I will look up at You confidently each time I find myself at an obscure point or at a thought that is difficult to express. I will come to You here often to ask for counsel in difficult circumstances; here, close to You, at the foot of Your picture, I will kneel down whenever I am sad or when temptation overcomes me. Here and nowhere else I will seek strength and consolation, instead of looking for it from worldly men or in outward pleasures.

Every evening I will render You here an accounting of my day.

O my Jesus, O my King, remember that I am Your priest, remember that I have received Your own spiritual authority and Your mission. Remember that the salvation of so many souls depends on my sanctification. I implore you: have pity on Your poor friend, who is so weak, and draw Him to Your burning Heart. Think of Your love, think of the souls; forget my unworthiness and let me enter into Your divine Heart. *O fornax ardens caritatis!*[593] Let me live there, be transformed there, be consumed in Your infinite love. Do not allow my occupation with external tasks, writing and working, separate my thoughts and my love from You. Do not allow me to return to my earlier distractions, to my nothingness, to my senselessness. Fill me with Your life, with Your love, with Your Spirit. Be the strength and light of my words when I speak or write; be the leader and organizer of my works, wherever I may be and wherever I go.

O my God, I wish so much to live and act in union with You! I wish so much to be so dependent on You in everything, that I can joyfully repeat: "I live, I write, I work, I am in trouble: *vivo ego,*[594] but no longer like a pagan, no longer like a faithless priest, nor like an unproductive worker full of self-confidence: *no, vivo ego, jam non ego.*[595] I no longer look to myself for guidance, I no longer rely on my own wisdom or my own strength; *vivit vero in me Christus.*[596] You are the one, O Christ, who lives and works in me; You are the one who directs everything and makes it all fruitful."

---

[593] O burning furnace of love.

[594] Gal. 2:20: "I live."

[595] *Ibid.*, "I live, now not I."

[596] *Ibid.*, "Christ liveth in me."

O Mary, my Queen and my Mother, O tender Mediatrix of all grace, I consecrate myself to you entirely with all that I am and all that I have. Share with me this life of grace, this life of Jesus with which you are full. Form in me the priest of Jesus, so that soon I may become with Jesus a sacrifice of love for souls, and so that all my prayers, works of penance and actions may be like the pleasing fragrance of my trusting, continual sacrifice.

Regina Cleri, ora pro nobis.
Cor Jesu eucharisticum, exemplar cordis sacerdotalis, miserere nobis.
Cor Jesu sacratissimum, adveniat Regnum tuum.

Cor Jesu, Cor amabile,
Amore nostri saucium,
Amore nostri languidum,
Fac sis mihi placabile.

Servus tuus in Maria,
Eduard Poppe, Presbyter
in festo B.M.V. de Monte Carmelo 1920.

Queen of the clergy, pray for us.
Eucharistic Heart of Jesus, example of the priestly heart, have mercy on us.
Sacred Heart of Jesus, Your kingdom come.

Heart of Jesus, lovable Heart,
Wounded for love of us,
Languishing for love of us,
Be merciful to me.

Your servant in Mary,
Eduard Poppe, Priest
On the Feast of Our Lady of Mount Carmel 1920.

Appendix Four

Excerpt From the Encyclical Annum Sacrum, With Commentary

On May 25, 1899, the Encyclical *Annum Sacrum* announced to the Christian people a great plan of Pope Leo XIII, from which he expected, if only everyone would comply with internal consent, great and lasting fruits, first for the Christian good name, and then also for the whole human race: *auctores suasoresque sumus praeclarae cujusdam rei, ex qua quidem, si modo omnes ex animo, si consentientibus libentibusque voluntatibus paruerint, primum quidem nomini christiano, deinde societati hominum universae fructus insignes non sine cause expectamus eosdemque mansuros.* He recalled what his predecessors had done for the Heart of Jesus and what he himself had undertaken. "But now," he added, "We have in mind a more signal form of devotion which shall be in a manner the crowning perfection of all the honors that people have been accustomed to pay to the Sacred Heart, and which We confidently trust will be most pleasing to Jesus Christ, our Redeemer": *"nunc vero luculentior quaedam obsequii forma obversatur animo quae scilicet honorum omnium, quotquot sacratissimo Cordi haberi consueverunt, velut absolutio perfectioque sit."*

He recalls the petitions that were addressed to Pius IX and the consecration in the year 1875. It seemed to him that the time has come finally to consecrate the whole human race to the Sacred Heart of Jesus, *communitatem generis humani devovere autustissimo Cordi Jesu.* He justified his decision by demonstrating the Jesus is the supreme King, the King not only of Catholics and of the baptized, but of the whole human race; and he indicated the title of His kingship. What he wants, however, is the voluntary, joyful acknowledgment of this kingship; the consecration is precisely this: "Since there is in the Sacred Heart a symbol and a sensible image of the infinite love of Jesus Christ which moves us to love one another, therefore is it fit and proper that we should consecrate ourselves to His most Sacred Heart—an act which is nothing else than an offering and a binding of oneself to Jesus Christ." But can we forget those who do not know Jesus? We send apostles to them everywhere; but "so now, in pity for their lot with all Our soul we commend them, and as far as in us lies We consecrate them to the Sacred Heart of Jesus. In this way this act of devotion, which We recommend, will be a blessing to all," since for some this consecration will increase their faith and love, while it draws down the graces of sanctification and salvation for the others. The Pope then shows that redemption is given to us for sick society. Centuries ago, he say, the Cross appeared to Constantine, an omen and at the same time the cause of his victory. "And now, today, behold another blessed and heavenly token *(auspicatissimum divinissimumque signum)* is offered to our sight—the most Sacred Heart of Jesus, with a cross rising from it and shining forth with dazzling splendor amidst flames of love. In that Sacred Heart all our hopes should be placed, and from it the salvation of men is to be confidently besought."

The Pope then says that in addition to these sublime reasons of a general order there is another reason of a more personal sort: God kept him alive by saving him from a serious illness; he for his part gratefully wished to commemorate this blessing by an increased reverence for the Sacred Heart of Jesus. He therefore ordered a triduum with prayers and the Litany to the Sacred Heart of Jesus, and he sent along with his Letter the prayer of consecration that was to be recited on the final day.

The Encyclical bore the date of May 25, 1899. Consequently there was no time to lose. But it had already been announced two months previously. Through the Decree dated April 2 the Sacred Congregation of Rites had permitted the public recitation of the Litany to the Sacred Heart. Among the points taken into consideration is this one: "Moreover His Holiness intended to consecrate the whole world to the Sacred Heart of Jesus. Now in order to lend a solemn character to this consecration, His Holiness decided to order in the near future a triduum during which this litany will be chanted." This announcement could scarcely come any sooner, because the decision was not made until March 25.

The Pope was thinking about having it during the year 1900. Probably the danger of death that he had just escaped, which is mentioned in the Encyclical, accelerated the event. But despite the haste, the Catholic world was prepared, and it is well known with what magnificent and at the same time fervent solemnity this act of Leo XIII was carried out, which he called the "greatest act" of his pontificate.

During First Vespers of this Feast of the Sacred Heart of Jesus, the External Solemnity of which had been transferred to a Sunday which was marked by this great act, a nun died in a cloister in Portugal, unknown to the world; from her had proceeded this enormous movement that caused the world to kneel at the feet of the Heart of Jesus. Here we have one of those facts that illuminate Church history with a special day; and although it is enjoyable to investigate the background of human events, even at the risk of finding only small-mindedness or violence, how much more joy is to be found in religious matters, if only we see, if only we know how to see the finger of God!

On June 10, 1898, a letter was sent to Leo XIII from Good Shepherd convent in Porto, Portugal. The nun who had signed it in pencil in a frail hand told the Pope that she had received from our Lord the command to write to him that His Vicar should consecrate the whole world to His divine Heart; He promised as a reward an outpouring of graces. They say that Leo XIII was moved but made no plans. Are there not crazed minds who often present their ideas to him, maintaining that they came from heaven? On January 6, 1899, a second letter written in French was dispatched, "at the express command of our Lord and with the approval of my father confessor." The letter read: "Last summer, when Your Holiness suffered from an indisposition which, in view of Your advanced age, filled the hearts of Your children with concern, our Lord gave me the sweet consolation that He would lengthen the days of Your Holiness so as to perform the consecration of the whole world to His divine Heart." Other details along the same lines followed. The letter continues: "On the eve of the Immaculate Conception, our Lord informed me that through this new beginning that devotion to His divine Heart will have, He will cause a new light to shine over the whole world.... It seemed to me as though I saw this light interiorly, the Heart of Jesus, this adorable sun that let its rays fall down upon the earth, at first more restrictedly, but then expanding and finally illuminating the whole world. And He said: From the splendor of the light the peoples and the nations will be enlightened and they will be warmed by its glow."

The letter then spoke about Jesus' desire to see His adorable Heart known and glorified more and more and to pour out His gifts and blessings upon the whole world; He spoke about the choice that had fallen to Leo XIII and the lengthening of his days with a view to this, and the graces that He would thereby obtain. "I feel unworthy," the letter continued, "to communicate all this to Your Holiness." But the writer excused herself by citing the "strict command" of our Lord. It was then explained why our Lord desires the consecration of the whole world and not only of the Catholic Church. "His desire to reign, to be loved and glorified, is so ardent that He wants Your Holiness to bring Him the hearts of all who belong to Him through Holy Baptism, so as to facilitate their return to the true Church, and so as to hasten by this means the spiritual birth of the hearts of those who have not yet received spiritual life through Holy Baptism yet for whom He gave up His life and His Blood and who are also called to be children of Holy Church someday." Then followed urgent appeals to the Pope to propagate devotion to the divine Heart: "Our Lord spoke to me directly only about the consecration. But it seems to me that it would be very pleasing to Him if the devotion of the First Fridays of the month were enriched by an admonition of Your Holiness to the clergy and the faithful, as well as by the granting of new indulgences. Our Lord," she repeated, "did not tell me this explicitly, as He spoke about the consecration, but I think that I can guess this ardent desire of His Heart without however being able to declare it." The letter was signed "Sister Maria of the Divine Heart Droste zu Vischering, Superior of the Cloister of the Good Shepherd in Porto."

This letter arrived at the Vatican on January 15. The Pope was moved. He commissioned Cardinal Jacobini to obtain more detailed information. The latter wrote to the Assistant Rector of the major seminary, who was the nun's spiritual director and had served as her secretary for the first letter to the Pope. The answer was that she was regarded everywhere as a saint and that there were good reasons to think that these were supernatural communications. Leo XIII was pleased, moreover, by the idea, and on February 12 he communicated to Msgr. Isoard his intention to consecrate all dioceses, the Church and mankind to the Sacred Heart. But he did not want this papal act to rely on a foundation that could be doubted. Cardinal Mazzella, Prefect of the Congregation of Rites, who was informed about everything, told the Pope: "This letter is extremely moving; it seems to have been dictated by our Lord." "Your Eminence," Leo XIII replied, "take it and set it aside; it must not count at this moment." The Cardinal was therefore commissioned to examine the question in itself. A difficulty arose: How could unbelievers, who are not part of the Church and do not belong to the Church, be consecrated? A passage from St. Thomas resolved the difficulties (III, q. 59, art. 4). It explains that, although not all belong to Jesus and the Church *quantum ad exsecutionem potestatis* [so far as concerns the execution of her authority], they nevertheless do belong to her *quantum ad potestatem* [so far as concerns her authority]. That was more or less what the nun had said. But the passage from St. Thomas fit exactly and found its place in the Encyclical. On Easter Sunday, April 3, when the Decree of the Sacred Congregation of Rites allowed [the public recitation of] the Litany to the Sacred Heart and announced the consecration, the Pope politely had two copies of the document sent to Mother Maria of the Divine Heart.

Three days before the consecration she passed away, like Margaret Mary, to be hidden forever in the abyss of the Most Sacred Heart of Jesus.

See also Louis Chaste, *Soeur Marie du Coeur Divin, née Droste zu Vischering, religieuse du Bon Pasteur, 1863-1899* (Paris, 1905),[597] Chapter 11, where the reader will find everything concerning the consecration of the human race to the Sacred Heart of Jesus.

The second wish of Mother Maria of the Divine Heart was fulfilled in the month following her death. On July 21 the Prefect of the Sacred Congregation of Rites, in the name of the Supreme Pontiff, addressed an urgent invitation to all the bishops to promote devotion to the Sacred Heart of Jesus through sodalities, through the Month of the Sacred Heart and through the practice of the First Fridays.

[Excerpt from the article *"Coeur Sacré de Jésus"* in the *Dictionnaire de Théologie Catholique*, cols. 340-343]

---

[597] The German edition, published by Herder, was adapted from the French edition while incorporating original texts in German by Fr. Leo Sasttler, O.S.B.

Appendix Five

Encyclical of Pope Pius XI dated May 8, 1928, *Miserentissimus Redemptor* (Excerpts)

I. The Heart of the Savior—Symbol of Love and Peace

Among the many proofs of the boundless benignity of our Redeemer, there is one that stands out conspicuously, to wit the fact that when the charity of Christian people was growing cold, the Divine Charity itself was set forth to be honored by a special worship, and the riches of its bounty was made widely manifest by that form of devotion wherein worship is given to the Most Sacred Heart of Jesus, "In whom are hid all the treasures of wisdom and knowledge."[598]

... And indeed Our Predecessor of happy memory, Leo XIII, admiring the timely opportuneness of the devotion to the Most Sacred Heart of Jesus, said very aptly in his Encyclical Letter, *Annum Sacrum,* "When in the days near her origin, the Church was oppressed under the yoke of the Caesars the Cross shown on high to the youthful Emperor was at once an omen and a cause of the victory that speedily followed. And here today another most auspicious and most divine sign is offered to our sight, to wit the most Sacred Heart of Jesus, with a Cross set above it shining with most resplendent brightness in the midst of flames. Herein must all hopes be set, from hence must the salvation of men be sought and expected."[599]

---

[598] Col. 2:3.

[599] Leo XIII, Encyclical *Annum Sacrum* (25 May 1899), ASS 31 (1899): 650-651.

❤ *Prototype of Divine Veneration and Summary of Religion*

And rightly indeed is that said, Venerable Brethren. For is not the sum of all religion and therefore the pattern of more perfect life, contained in that most auspicious sign and in the form of piety that follows from it...?

II. Forms of Devotion to the Heart of Jesus

1. Consecration

But assuredly among those things which properly pertain to the worship of the Most Sacred Heart, a special place must be given to that Consecration, whereby we devote ourselves and all things that are ours to the Divine Heart of Jesus, acknowledging that we have received all things from the everlasting love of God. When Our Savior had taught Margaret Mary, the most innocent disciple of His Heart, how much He desired that this duty of devotion should be rendered to him by men, moved in this not so much by His own right as by His immense charity for us; she herself, with her spiritual father, Claude de la Colombière, rendered it the first of all.

... But since in the last century, and in this present century, things have come to such a pass, that by the machinations of wicked men the sovereignty of Christ Our Lord has been denied and war is publicly waged against the Church, by passing laws and promoting plebiscites repugnant to Divine and natural law, nay more by holding assemblies of them that cry out, "We will not have this man to reign over us":[600] from the aforesaid Consecration there burst forth over against them in keenest opposition the voice of all the clients of the Most Sacred Heart, as it were one voice, to vindicate His glory and to assert His rights: "Christ must reign";[601] "Thy kingdom come."[602] From this at length it happily came to pass that at the beginning of this century the whole human race which Christ, in whom all things are re-established,[603] possesses by native

---

[600] Lk. 19:14.
[601] 1Cor. 15:25.
[602] Mt. 6:10.
[603] Cf. Eph. 1:10.

right as His own, was dedicated to the same Most Sacred Heart, with the applause of the whole Christian world, by Our Predecessor of happy memory, Leo XIII.[604] ...

2. Reparation

But to all these duties, more especially to that fruitful Consecration which was in a manner confirmed by the sacred solemnity of Christ the King, something else must needs be added, and it is concerning this that it is Our pleasure to speak with you more at length, Venerable Brethren, on the present occasion: we mean that duty of honorable satisfaction or reparation which must be rendered to the Most Sacred Heart of Jesus. For if the first and foremost thing in Consecration is this, that the creature's love should be given in return for the love of the Creator, another thing follows from this at once, namely that to the same uncreated Love, if so be it has been neglected by forgetfulness or violated by offense, some sort of compensation must be rendered for the injury, and this debt is commonly called by the name of reparation.

a) Reparation a matter of justice

Now though in both these matters we are impelled by quite the same motives, none the less we are holden to the duty of reparation and expiation by a certain more valid title of justice and of love, of justice indeed, in order that the offense offered to God by our sins may be expiated and that the violated order may be repaired by penance: it is a matter of love too, so that we may suffer together with Christ suffering and "filled with reproaches" (Lam. 3:30), and for all our poverty may offer Him some little solace.

For since we are all sinners and laden with many faults, our God must be honored by us not only by that worship wherewith we adore His infinite Majesty with due homage, or acknowledge His supreme dominion by praying, or praise His boundless bounty

---

[604] Cf. Leo XIII, Encyclical *Annum Sacrum* (25 May 1899), *ASS* (1899): 651.

by thanksgiving; but besides this we must need make satisfaction to God the just avenger, "for our numberless sins and offenses and negligences." To Consecration, therefore, whereby we are devoted to God and are called holy to God, by that holiness and stability which, as the Angelic Doctor teaches, is proper to consecration,[605] there must be added expiation, whereby sins are wholly blotted out, lest the holiness of the supreme justice may punish our shameless unworthiness, and reject our offering as hateful rather than accept it as pleasing.

❤ *The Necessity of Reparation*

Moreover this duty of expiation is laid upon the whole race of men since, as we are taught by the Christian faith, after Adam's miserable fall, infected by hereditary stain, subject to concupiscences and most wretchedly depraved, it would have been thrust down into eternal destruction....

❤ *Through Christ's Sacrifice on the Cross*

But no created power was sufficient to expiate the sins of men, if the Son of God had not assumed man's nature in order to redeem it. This, indeed, the Savior of men Himself declared by the mouth of the sacred Psalmist: "Sacrifice and oblation thou wouldst not: but a body thou hast fitted to me: Holocausts for sin did not please thee: then said I: Behold I come."[606] And in very deed, "Surely He hath borne our infirmities, and carried our sorrows.... He was wounded for our iniquities,"[607] and "He His own self bore our sins in His body upon the tree."[608] "Blotting out the handwriting of the decree that was against us, which was contrary to us. And He has taken the same out of the way, fastening it to the cross...,"[609] "that we being dead to sins, should live to justice."[610]

---

[605] Cf. Thomas Aquinas, Summa Theologiae, II-II, q. 81, art. 8.
[606] Heb. 10:5-7.
[607] Isa. 53:4-5.
[608] 1Pet. 2:24.
[609] Col. 2:14.
[610] 1Pet. 2:24.

♥ *Our Cooperation Through Sharing in Christ's sufferings*

Yet, though the copious redemption of Christ has abundantly forgiven us all offenses,[611] nevertheless, because of that wondrous divine dispensation whereby those things that are wanting of the sufferings of Christ are to be filled up in our flesh for His body which is the Church,[612] to the praises and satisfactions, "which Christ in the name of sinners rendered unto God" we can also add our praises and satisfactions, and indeed it behooves us so to do. But we must ever remember that the whole virtue of the expiation depends on the one bloody sacrifice of Christ, which without intermission of time is renewed on our altars in an unbloody manner. "For the victim is one and the same, the same now offering by the ministry of priests, who then offered Himself on the cross, the manner alone of offering being different."[613] Wherefore with this most august Eucharistic Sacrifice there ought to be joined an oblation both of the ministers and of all the faithful, so that they also may "present themselves living sacrifices, holy, pleasing unto God."[614] Nay more, St. Cyprian does not hesitate to affirm that "the Lord's sacrifice is not celebrated with legitimate sanctification, unless our oblation and sacrifice correspond to His passion."[615] ...

Nor do those only enjoy a participation in this mystic priesthood and in the office of satisfying and sacrificing, whom our Pontiff Christ Jesus uses as His ministers to offer up the clean oblation to God's Name in every place from the rising of the sun to the going down,[616] but the whole Christian people rightly called by the Prince of the Apostles "a chosen generation, a kingly priesthood"[617] ought to offer for sins both for itself and for all mankind,[618] in much the same manner as every priest and pontiff "taken from among men, is ordained for men in the things that appertain to God."[619]

---

[611] Cf. Col. 2:13.

[612] Cf. Col. 1:24.

[613] Council of Trent, Session XXIII, Chapter 2. Denzinger no. 940.

[614] Rom. 12:1.

[615] Cyprian, *Epist.* LXIII, 9; PL 4:381.

[616] Cf. Mal. 1:11.

[617] 1 Pet. 2:9.

[618] Cf. Heb. 5:3.

[619] Heb. 5:1.

But the more perfectly that our oblation and sacrifice corresponds to the sacrifice of Our Lord, that is to say, the more perfectly we have immolated our love and our desires and have crucified our flesh by that mystic crucifixion of which the Apostle speaks, the more abundant fruits of that propitiation and expiation shall we receive for ourselves and for others. For there is a wondrous and close union of all the faithful with Christ, such as that which prevails between the Head and the other members; moreover by that mystic Communion of Saints which we profess in the Catholic creed, both individual men and peoples are joined together not only with one another but also with him, "who is the head, Christ."[620]

b) The Motive of Love

Wherefore, even as consecration proclaims and confirms this union with Christ, so does expiation begin that same union by washing away faults, and perfect it by participating in the sufferings of Christ, and consummate it by offering victims for the brethren. And this indeed was the purpose of the merciful Jesus, when He showed His Heart to us bearing about it the symbols of the passion and displaying the flames of love, that from the one we might know the infinite malice of sin, and in the other we might admire the infinite charity of our Redeemer, and so might have a more vehement hatred of sin, and make a more ardent return of love for His love.

❤ The Savior Demands Reparation

And truly the spirit of expiation or reparation has always had the first and foremost place in the worship given to the Most Sacred Heart of Jesus, and nothing is more in keeping with the origin, the character, the power, and the distinctive practices of this form of devotion, as appears from the record of history and custom, as well as from the sacred liturgy and the acts of the Sovereign Pontiffs. For when Christ manifested Himself to Margaret Mary, and declared to her the infinitude of His love, at the same time, in the manner of a mourner, He complained that so many and such great injuries were done to Him by ungrateful men—and we would that these

---

[620] Eph. 4:15.

words in which He made this complaint were fixed in the minds of the faithful, and were never blotted out by oblivion: "Behold this Heart," He said, "which has loved men so much and has loaded them with all benefits, and for this boundless love has had no return but neglect, and contumely, and this often from those who were bound by a debt and duty of a more special love."

In order that these faults might be washed away, He then recommended several things to be done, and in particular the following as most pleasing to Himself, namely that men should approach the Altar with this purpose of expiating sin, making what is called a Communion of Reparation, and that they should likewise make expiatory supplications and prayers, prolonged for a whole hour, which is rightly called the "Holy Hour." These pious exercises have been approved by the Church and have also been enriched with copious indulgences.

But how can these rites of expiation bring solace now, when Christ is already reigning in the beatitude of Heaven? To this we may answer in some words of St. Augustine which are very apposite here: "Give me one who loves, and he will understand what I say."[621]

♥ Christ's Suffering

For any one who has great love of God, if he will look back through the tract of past time may dwell in meditation on Christ, and see Him laboring for man, sorrowing, suffering the greatest hardships, "for us men and for our salvation," well-nigh worn out with sadness, with anguish, nay "bruised for our sins"[622] and healing us by His bruises. And the minds of the pious meditate on all these things the more truly, because the sins of men and their crimes committed in every age were the cause why Christ was delivered up to death, and now also they would of themselves bring death to Christ, joined with the same griefs and sorrows, since each several sin in its own way is held to renew the passion of Our Lord: "Crucifying again to themselves the Son of God, and making him a mockery."[623]

---

[621] Augustine, *In Johannis Evangelium,* tract. XXVI, 4; PL 35, 1608.

[622] Isa. 53:5.

[623] Heb. 6:6.

Now if, because of our sins also which were as yet in the future, but were foreseen, the soul of Christ became sorrowful unto death, it cannot be doubted that then, too, already He derived somewhat of solace from our reparation, which was likewise foreseen, when "there appeared to Him an angel from heaven,"[624] in order that His Heart, oppressed with weariness and anguish, might find consolation. And so even now, in a wondrous yet true manner, we can and ought to console that Most Sacred Heart which is continually wounded by the sins of thankless men, since—as we also read in the sacred liturgy—Christ Himself, by the mouth of the Psalmist complains that He is forsaken by His friends: "My Heart hath expected reproach and misery, and I looked for one that would grieve together with me, but there was none: and for one that would comfort me, and I found none."[625]

c) Urgency of Reparation Today
♥ The Persecuted Church

Now, how great is the necessity of this expiation or reparation, more especially in this our age, will be manifest to every one who, as we said at the outset, will examine the world, "seated in wickedness",[626] with his eyes and with his mind. For from all sides the cry of the peoples who are mourning comes up to us, and their princes or rulers have indeed stood up and met together in one against the Lord and against His Church.[627] Throughout those regions indeed, we see that all rights both human and Divine are confounded.... These things in truth are so sad that you might say that such events foreshadow and portend the "beginning of sorrows",[628] that is to say of those that shall be brought by the man of sin, "who is lifted up above all that is called God or is worshipped."[629]

---

[624] Lk. 22:43.
[625] Ps. 68:21.
[626] 1Jn. 5:19.
[627] Cf. Ps. 2:2.
[628] Mt. 24:8.
[629] 2Thess. 2:4.

❤ *Deplorable Abuses Among Christians*

But it is yet more to be lamented, Venerable Brethren, that among the faithful themselves, washed in Baptism with the blood of the immaculate Lamb, and enriched with grace, there are found so many men of every class, who laboring under an incredible ignorance of Divine things and infected with false doctrines, far from their Father's home, lead a life involved in vices, a life which is not brightened by the light of true faith, nor gladdened by the hope of future beatitude, nor refreshed and cherished by the fire of charity; so that they truly seem to sit in darkness and in the shadow of death. Moreover, among the faithful there is a greatly increasing carelessness of ecclesiastical discipline, and of those ancient institutions on which all Christian life rests, by which domestic society is governed, and the sanctity of marriage is safeguarded; the education of children is altogether neglected, or else it is depraved by too indulgent blandishments, and the Church is even robbed of the power of giving the young a Christian education; there is a sad forgetfulness of Christian modesty especially in the life and the dress of women; there is an unbridled cupidity of transitory things, a want of moderation in civic affairs, an unbounded ambition of popular favor, a depreciation of legitimate authority, and lastly a contempt for the word of God, whereby faith itself is injured, or is brought into proximate peril.

❤ *Abuses Among the Clergy and Consecrated Religious*

But all these evils as it were culminate in the cowardice and the sloth of those who, after the manner of the sleeping and fleeing disciples, wavering in their faith, miserably forsake Christ when He is oppressed by anguish or surrounded by the satellites of Satan, and in the perfidy of those others who following the example of the traitor Judas, either partake of the holy table rashly and sacrilegiously, or go over to the camp of the enemy. And thus, even against our will, the thought rises in the mind that now those days draw near of which Our Lord prophesied: "Because iniquity hath abounded, the charity of many shall grow cold."[630]

---

[630] Mt. 24:12.

❤ *The Spirit of Reparation*

Now, whosoever of the faithful have piously pondered on all these things must need be inflamed with the charity of Christ in His agony and make a more vehement endeavor to expiate their own faults and those of others, to repair the honor of Christ, and to promote the eternal salvation of souls. And indeed that saying of the Apostle: "Where sin abounded, grace did more abound,"[631] may be used in a manner to describe this present age; for while the wickedness of men has been greatly increased, at the same time, by the inspiration of the Holy Ghost, a marvelous increase has been made in the number of the faithful of both sexes who with eager mind endeavor to make satisfaction for the many injuries offered to the Divine Heart, nay more they do not hesitate to offer themselves to Christ as victims.

For indeed if any one will lovingly dwell on those things of which we have been speaking, and will have them deeply fixed in his mind, it cannot be but he will shrink with horror from all sin as from the greatest evil, and more than this he will yield himself wholly to the will of God, and will strive to repair the injured honor of the Divine Majesty, as well by constantly praying, as by voluntary mortifications, by patiently bearing the afflictions that befall him, and lastly by spending his whole life in this exercise of expiation....

❤ *The Feast of the Sacred Heart of Jesus, an Occasion to Make Reparation*

These things being so, Venerable Brethren, just as the rite of consecration, starting from humble beginnings, and afterwards more widely propagated, was at length crowned with success by Our confirmation; so in like manner, we earnestly desire that this custom of expiation or pious reparation, long since devoutly introduced and devoutly propagated, may also be more firmly sanctioned by Our Apostolic authority and more solemnly celebrated by the whole Catholic name.

Wherefore, we decree and command that every year on the Feast of the Most Sacred Heart of Jesus, ... in all churches throughout the whole world, the same expiatory prayer or protestation as it is called, to Our most loving Savior, set forth in the same words according to

---

[631] Rom. 5:20.

the copy subjoined to this letter shall be solemnly recited, so that all our faults may be washed away with tears, and reparation may be made for the violated rights of Christ the supreme King and our most loving Lord.

❤ *The Anticipated Good Fruits*

There is surely no reason for doubting, Venerable Brethren, that from this devotion piously established and commanded to the whole Church, many excellent benefits will flow forth not only to individual men but also to society, sacred, civil, and domestic, seeing that our Redeemer Himself promised to Margaret Mary that "all those who rendered this honor to His Heart would be endowed with an abundance of heavenly graces. Sinners indeed, looking on Him whom they pierced,[632] moved by the sighs and tears of the whole Church, by grieving for the injuries offered to the supreme King, will return to the heart,[633] lest perchance being hardened in their faults, when they see Him whom they pierced "coming in the clouds of heaven",[634] too late and in vain they shall bewail themselves because of Him.[635] But the just shall be justified and shall be sanctified still,[636] and they will devote themselves wholly and with new ardor to the service of their King, when they see Him contemned and attacked and assailed with so many and such great insults, but more than all will they burn with zeal for the eternal salvation of souls when they have pondered on the complaint of the Divine Victim: "What profit is there in my blood?"[637] and likewise on the joy that will be felt by the same Most Sacred Heart of Jesus "upon one sinner doing penance."[638] And this indeed we more especially and vehemently desire and confidently expect, that the just and merciful God who would have spared Sodom for the sake

---

[632] Jn. 19:37.
[633] Isa. 46:8.
[634] Mt. 26:64.
[635] Cf. Apoc. 1:7.
[636] Cf. Apoc. 22:11.
[637] Ps. 29:10.
[638] Lk. 15:10.

of ten just men, will much more be ready to spare the whole race of men, when He is moved by the humble petitions and happily appeased by the prayers of the community of the faithful praying together in union with Christ their Mediator and Head, in the name of all.

Conclusion: Mary, the Model of Reparation

And now lastly may the most benign Virgin Mother of God smile on this purpose and on these desires of ours; for since she brought forth for us Jesus our Redeemer, and nourished Him, and offered Him as a victim by the Cross, by her mystic union with Christ and His very special grace she likewise became and is piously called a Reparatrix. Trusting in her intercession with Christ, who whereas He is the "one mediator of God and men",[639] chose to make His Mother the advocate of sinners, and the minister and Mediatrix of grace, as an earnest of heavenly gifts and as a token of Our paternal affection we most lovingly impart the Apostolic Blessing to you, Venerable Brethren, and to all the flock committed to your care.

Given at Rome, at St. Peter's, on the eighth day of May, 1928, in the seventh year of Our Pontificate.

POPE PIUS XI

---

[639] 1 Tim. 2:5.

Prayer of Reparation

O sweetest Jesus, whose overflowing charity towards men is most ungratefully repaid by such great forgetfulness, neglect and contempt, see, prostrate before Thy altars, we strive by special honor to make amends for the wicked coldness of men and the contumely with which Thy most loving Heart is everywhere treated.

At the same time, mindful of the fact that we too have sometimes not been free from unworthiness, and moved therefore with most vehement sorrow, in the first place we implore Thy mercy on us, being prepared by voluntary expiation to make amends for the sins we have ourselves committed, and also for the sins of those who wander far from the way of salvation, whether because, being obstinate in their unbelief, they refuse to follow Thee as their shepherd and leader, or because, spurning the promises of their Baptism, they have cast off the most sweet yoke of Thy law.

We now endeavor to expiate all these lamentable crimes together, and it is also our purpose to make amends for each one of them severally: for the want of modesty in life and dress, for impurities, for so many snares set for the minds of the innocent, for the violation of feast days, for the horrid blasphemies against Thee and Thy saints, for the insults offered to Thy Vicar and to the priestly order, for the neglect of the Sacrament of Divine love or its profanation by horrible sacrileges, and lastly for the public sins of nations which resist the rights and the teaching authority of the Church which Thou hast instituted.

Would that we could wash away these crimes with our own blood! And now, to make amends for the outrage offered to the Divine honor, we offer to Thee the same satisfaction which Thou didst once offer to Thy Father on the Cross and which Thou dost continually renew on our altars, we offer this conjoined with the expiations of the Virgin Mother and of all the Saints, and of all pious Christians, promising from our heart that so far as in us lies, with the help of Thy grace, we will make amends for our own past sins, and for the sins of others, and for the neglect of Thy boundless love, by firm faith, by a pure way of life, and by a perfect observance of the Gospel law, especially that of charity; we will also strive with all our strength to prevent injuries being offered to Thee, and gather as many as we can to become Thy followers. Receive, we beseech Thee, O most benign Jesus, by the intercession of the Blessed Virgin Mary, the Reparatrix, the voluntary homage of this expiation, and vouchsafe, by that great gift of final perseverance, to keep us most faithful until death in our duty and in Thy service, so that at length we may all come to that fatherland, where Thou with the Father and the Holy Ghost livest and reignest God for ever and ever. Amen.

Appendix Six

Encyclical of Pope Pius XII *Haurietis Aquas* on Devotion to The Sacred Heart [Excerpts]

Introduction: Devotion to the Heart of Jesus, a Source of the Richest Graces

2. It is altogether impossible to enumerate the heavenly gifts which devotion to the Sacred Heart of Jesus has poured out on the souls of the faithful, purifying them, offering them heavenly strength, rousing them to the attainment of all virtues. Therefore, recalling those wise words of the Apostle St. James, "Every best gift and every perfect gift is from above, coming down from the Father of Lights,"[640] We are perfectly justified in seeing in this same devotion, which flourishes with increasing fervor throughout the world, a gift without price which our divine Savior the Incarnate Word, as the one Mediator of grace and truth between the heavenly Father and the human race imparted to the Church, His mystical Spouse, in recent centuries when she had to endure such trials and surmount so many difficulties.

3. The Church, rejoicing in this inestimable gift, can show forth a more ardent love of her divine Founder, and can, in a more generous and effective manner, respond to that invitation which St. John the Evangelist relates as having come from Christ Himself: "And on the last and great day of the festivity, Jesus stood and cried out, saying, 'If any man thirst, let him come to Me, and let him drink that believeth in Me. As the Scripture saith: Out of his heart

---

[640] Jas. 1:17.

there shall flow rivers of living waters.' Now this He said of the Spirit which they should receive who believed in Him."[641]

The Nature of This Devotion

5. Divine Love first takes its origin from the Holy Spirit, Who is the Love in Person of the Father and the Son in the bosom of the most Holy Trinity. Most aptly then does the Apostle of the Gentiles echo, as it were, the words of Jesus Christ, when he ascribes the pouring forth of love in the hearts of believers to this Spirit of Love: "The charity of God is poured forth in our hearts by the Holy Spirit Who is given to us."[642]

6. Holy Writ declares that between divine charity, which must burn in the souls of Christians, and the Holy Spirit, Who is certainly Love itself, there exists the closest bond, which clearly shows all of us, Venerable Brethren, the intimate nature of that worship which must be paid to the Most Sacred Heart of Jesus Christ. If we consider its special nature it is beyond question that this devotion is an act of religion of high order; it demands of us a complete and unreserved determination to devote and consecrate ourselves to the love of the divine Redeemer, Whose wounded Heart is its living token and symbol. It is equally clear, but at a higher level, that this same devotion provides us with a most powerful means of repaying the divine Lord by our own.

7. Indeed it follows that it is only under the impulse of love that the minds of men obey fully and perfectly the rule of the Supreme Being, since the influence of our love draws us close to the divine Will that it becomes as it were completely one with it, according to the saying, "He who is joined to the Lord, is one spirit."[643]

---

[641] Jn. 7:37-39. (Translator's note: In this passage, Pope Pius XII uses the punctuation favored by St. Irenaeus and St. Cyprian and some other ancient authorities. The translation therefore follows this and not the Douay version.)

[642] Rom. 5:15.

[643] 1Cor. 6:17.

The Heart of Jesus and His mission as Redeemer

1. The Love of Jesus Christ

62. And now, Venerable Brethren, in order that we may be able to gather from these holy considerations abundant and salutary fruits, We desire to reflect on and briefly contemplate the manifold affections, human and divine, of our Savior Jesus Christ which His Heart made known to us during the course of His mortal life and which it still does and will continue to do for all eternity. From the pages of the Gospel particularly there shines forth for us the light, by the brightness and strength of which we can enter into the secret places of this divine Heart and, with the Apostle of the Gentiles, gaze at "the abundant riches of (God's) grace, in his bounty towards us in Christ Jesus."[644]

a) At the First Moment of His Incarnation

63. The adorable Heart of Jesus Christ began to beat with a love at once human and divine after the Virgin Mary generously pronounced Her "Fiat"; and the Word of God, as the Apostle remarks: "coming into the world, saith, 'Sacrifice and oblation thou wouldst not; but a body thou hast fitted to Me; holocausts for sin did not please thee. Then said I, "Behold I come"; in the head of the book it is written of Me, "that I should do thy will, O God!" '. . .In which will we are sanctified by the oblation of the body of Jesus Christ once."[645]

64. Likewise was He moved by love, completely in harmony with the affections of His human will and the divine Love, when in the house of Nazareth He conversed with His most sweet Mother and His foster father, St. Joseph, in obedience to whom He performed laborious tasks in the trade of a carpenter.

---

[644] Eph. 2:7.
[645] Heb. 10:5-7, 10.

b) During His Public Ministry

65. Again, He was influenced by that threefold love, of which We spoke, during His public life: in long apostolic journeys; in the working of innumerable miracles, by which He summoned back the dead from the grave or granted health to all manner of sick persons; in enduring labors; in bearing fatigue, hunger and thirst; in the nightly watchings during which He prayed most lovingly to His Father; and finally, in His preaching and in setting forth and explaining His parables, in those particularly which deal with mercy—the lost drachma, the lost sheep, the prodigal son. By these indeed both by act and by word, as St. Gregory the Great notes, the Heart of God itself is revealed: "Learn the Heart of God in the words of God, that you may long more ardently for things eternal."[646]

c) In His Words

66. But the Heart of Jesus Christ was moved by a more urgent charity when from His lips were drawn words breathing the most ardent love. Thus, to give examples: when He was gazing at the crowds weary and hungry, He exclaimed: "I have compassion upon the crowd";[647] and when He looked down on His beloved city of Jerusalem, blinded by its sins, and so destined for final ruin, He uttered this sentence: "Jerusalem, Jerusalem, thou that slayest the prophets, and stonest them that are sent unto thee, how often would I have gathered together thy children, as the hen doth gather her chickens under her wings, and thou wouldst not!"[648] And His Heart beat with love for His Father and with a holy anger when seeing the sacrilegious buying and selling taking place in the Temple, He rebuked the violators with these words: "It is written: My house shall be called a house of prayer; but you have made it a den of thieves."[649]

---

[646] Registr. epist., lib. IV, ep. 31, ad Theodorum medicum: P.L. LXXVII, 706.

[647] Mk. 8:2.

[648] Mt. 23:37.

[649] Mt. 21:13.

d) *During His Passion*

67. But His Heart was moved by a particularly intense love mingled with fear as He perceived the hour of His bitter torments drawing near and, expressing a natural repugnance for the approaching pains and death, He cried out: "Father, if it be possible, let this chalice pass from Me."[650] And when He was greeted by the traitor with a kiss, in love triumphant united to deepest grief, He addressed to him those words which seem to be the final invitation of His most merciful Heart to the friend who, obdurate in his wicked treachery, was about to hand Him over to His executioners: "Friend, whereto art thou come? Dost thou betray the Son of Man with a kiss?"[651] It was out of pity and the depths of His love that He spoke to the devout women as they wept for Him on His way to the unmerited penalty of the Cross: "Daughters of Jerusalem, weep not over Me, but weep for yourselves and for your children...For if in the green wood they do these things, what shall be done in the dry?"[652]

68. And when the divine Redeemer was hanging on the Cross, He showed that His Heart was strongly moved by different emotions—burning love, desolation, pity, longing desire, unruffled peace. The words spoken plainly indicate these emotions: "Father, forgive them; they know not what they do!"[653] "My God, My God, why hast Thou forsaken Me?"[654] "Amen, I say to thee, this day thou shalt be with Me in paradise."[655] "I thirst."[656] "Father, into Thy hands I commend My spirit."[657]

2. The Priceless Gifts of His Love

a) *The Most Blessed Sacrament*

69. But who can worthily depict those beatings of the divine Heart, the signs of His infinite love, of those moments when He granted men His greatest gifts: Himself in the Sacrament of the

---

[650] Mt. 26:39.
[651] Mt. 26:50; Lk. 22:48.
[652] Lk. 23:28, 31.
[653] Lk. 23:34.
[654] Mt. 27:46.
[655] Lk. 23:43.
[656] Jn. 19:28.
[657] Lk. 23:46.

Eucharist, His most holy Mother, and the office of the priesthood shared with us?

70. Even before He ate the Last Supper with His disciples Christ Our Lord, since He knew He was about to institute the sacrament of His body and blood by the shedding of which the new covenant was to be consecrated, felt His heart roused by strong emotions, which He revealed to the Apostles in these words: "With desire have I desired to eat this Pasch with you before I suffer."[658] And these emotions were doubtless even stronger when "taking bread, He gave thanks, and broke, and gave to them, saying, 'This is My body which is given for you, this do in commemoration of Me.' Likewise the chalice also, after He had supped, saying, 'This chalice is the new testament in My blood, which shall be shed for you.'"[659]

71. It can therefore be declared that the divine Eucharist, both the sacrament which He gives to men and the sacrifice in which He unceasingly offers Himself from the rising of the sun till the going down thereof,"[660] and likewise the priesthood, are indeed gifts of the Sacred Heart of Jesus.

b) His Most Holy Mother

72. Another most precious gift of His Sacred Heart is, as We have said, Mary the beloved Mother of God and the most loving Mother of us all. She who gave birth to our Savior according to the flesh and was associated with Him in recalling the children of Eve to the life of divine grace has deservedly been hailed as the spiritual Mother of the whole human race. And so St. Augustine writes of her: "Clearly She is Mother of the members of the Savior (which is what we are), because She labored with Him in love that the faithful who are members of the Head might be born in the Church."[661]

c) The Holy Sacrifice of the Mass

73. To the unbloody gift of Himself under the appearance of bread and wine our Savior Jesus Christ wished to join, as the

---

[658] Lk. 22:15.

[659] Lk. 22:19-20.

[660] Mal. 1:11.

[661] *De sancta virginitate,* VI, in: P.L. XL, 399.

chief proof of His deep and infinite love, the bloody sacrifice of the Cross. By this manner of acting He gave an example of His supreme charity, which He had proposed to His disciples as the highest point of love in these words: "Greater love than this no man hath, that a man lay down his life for his friends."[662]

74. Thus the love of Jesus Christ the Son of God, by the sacrifice of Golgotha, cast a flood of light on the meaning of the love of God Himself: "In this we know the charity of God, because He hath laid down His life for us, and we ought to lay down our lives for the brethren."[663] And in truth it was more by love than by the violence of the executioners that our divine Redeemer was fixed to the Cross; and His voluntary total offering is the supreme gift which He gave to each man, according to that terse saying of the Apostle, "He loved me, and delivered Himself for me."[664]

d) *The Church and the Sacraments*

75. The Sacred Heart of Jesus shares in a most intimate way in the life of the Incarnate Word, and has been thus assumed as a kind of instrument of the Divinity. It is therefore beyond all doubt that, in the carrying out of works of grace and divine omnipotence, His Heart, no less than the other members of His human nature is also a legitimate symbol of that unbounded love.[665]

76. Under the influence of this love, our Savior, by the outpouring of His blood, became wedded to His Church: "By love, He allowed Himself to be espoused to His Church."[666] Hence, from the wounded Heart of the Redeemer was born the Church, the dispenser of the Blood of the Redemption—whence flows that plentiful stream of Sacramental grace from which the children of the Church drink of eternal life, as we read in the sacred liturgy: "From the pierced Heart, the Church, the Bride of Christ, is born....And He pours forth grace from His Heart."[667]

---

[662] Jn. 15:13.

[663] 1Jn. 3:16.

[664] Gal. 2:20.

[665] Cf. *Summa Theologiae* III, q. 19, art. 1.

[666] *Summa Theologiae,* Suppl. Q. 42, art. 1 ad 3.

[667] Hymn at Vespers on the Feast of the Sacred Heart of Jesus.

77. Concerning the meaning of this symbol, which was known even to the earliest Fathers and ecclesiastical writers, St. Thomas Aquinas, echoing something of their words, writes as follows: "From the side of Christ, there flowed water for cleansing, blood for redeeming. Hence blood is associated with the sacrament of the Eucharist, water with the sacrament of Baptism, which has its cleansing power by virtue of the blood of Christ."[668]

78. What is here written of the side of Christ, opened by the wound from the soldier, should also be said of the Heart which was certainly reached by the stab of the lance, since the soldier pierced it precisely to make certain that Jesus Christ crucified was really dead. Hence the wound of the most Sacred Heart of Jesus, now that He has completed His mortal life, remains through the course of the ages a striking image of that spontaneous charity by which God gave His only begotten Son for the redemption of men and by which Christ expressed such passionate love for us that He offered Himself as a bleeding victim on Calvary for our sake: "Christ loved us and delivered Himself for us, an oblation and a sacrifice to God for an odor of sweetness."[669]

e) *The Continuation of These gifts in His glorified Body*

79. After our Lord had ascended into heaven with His Body adorned with the splendors of eternal glory and took His place by the right hand of the Father, He did not cease to remain with His Spouse, the Church, by means of the burning love with which His Heart beats. For He bears in His hands, feet and side the glorious marks of the wounds which manifest the threefold victory won over the devil, sin, and death.

80. He likewise keeps in His Heart, locked as it were in a most precious shrine, the unlimited treasures of His merits, the fruits of that same threefold triumph, which He generously bestows on the redeemed human race. This is a truth full of consolation, which the Apostle of the Gentiles expresses in these words: "Ascending on high, He led captivity captive; He gave gifts to men.... He that descended, is the same also that ascended above all the heavens that He might fill all things."[670]

---

[668] *Summa Theologiae*, III, q. 66, art. 3.

[669] Eph. 5:2.

[670] Eph. 4:8, 10.

f) *The Mission of the Holy Ghost*

81. The gift of the Holy Spirit, sent upon His disciples, is the first notable sign of His abounding charity after His triumphant ascent to the right hand of His Father. For after ten days the Holy Spirit, given by the heavenly Father, came down upon them gathered in the Upper Room in accordance with the promise made at the Last Supper: "I will ask the Father and He will give you another Paraclete so that He may abide with you forever."[671] And this Paraclete, who is the mutual personal love between the Father and the Son, is sent by both and, under the adopted appearance of tongues of fire, poured into their souls an abundance of divine charity and the other heavenly gifts.

82. The infusion of this divine charity also has its origin in the Heart of the Savior, "in which are hid all the treasures of wisdom and knowledge."[672] For this charity is the gift of Jesus Christ and of His Spirit; for He is indeed the spirit of the Father and the Son from whom the origin of the Church and its marvelous extension is revealed to all the pagan races which had been defiled by idolatry, family hatred, corrupt morals, and violence.

83. This divine charity is the most precious gift of the Heart of Christ and of His Spirit: It is this which imparted to the Apostles and martyrs that fortitude, by the strength of which they fought their battles like heroes till death in order to preach the truth of the Gospel and bear witness to it by the shedding of their blood; it is this which implanted in the Doctors of the Church their intense zeal for explaining and defending the Catholic faith; this nourished the virtues of the confessors, and roused them to those marvelous works useful for their own salvation and beneficial to the salvation of others both in this life and in the next; this, finally, moved the virgins to a free and joyful withdrawal from the pleasures of the senses and to the complete dedication of themselves to the love of their heavenly Spouse.

84. It was to pay honor to this divine charity which, overflowing from the Heart of the Incarnate Word, is poured out by the aid of the Holy Spirit into the souls of all believers that the Apostle of the Gentiles uttered this hymn of triumph which proclaims the victory of Christ the Head, and of the members of His Mystical Body,

---

[671] Jn. 14:16.
[672] Col. 2:3.

over all which might in any way impede the establishment of the kingdom of love among men: "Who shall separate us from the love of Christ? Shall tribulation or distress? or famine? or nakedness? or danger? or persecution? or the sword? . . . But in all these things we overcome because of Him that hath loved us. For I am sure that neither death nor life, nor angels nor principalities, nor powers, nor things present, nor things to come, nor might, nor height nor depth, nor any other creature shall be able to separate us from the love of God, which is in Christ Jesus our Lord."[673]

3. The legitimacy of Devotion to the Heart of Jesus

a) As Symbol of Christ's Love

85. Nothing therefore prevents our adoring the Sacred Heart of Jesus Christ as having a part in and being the natural and expressive symbol of the abiding love with which the divine Redeemer is still on fire for mankind. Though it is no longer subject to the varying emotions of this mortal life, yet it lives and beats and is united inseparably with the Person of the divine Word and, in Him and through Him, with the divine Will. Since then the Heart of Christ is overflowing with love both human and divine and rich with the treasure of all graces which our Redeemer acquired by His life, sufferings and death, it is therefore the enduring source of that charity which His Spirit pours forth on all the members of His Mystical Body.

b) As the Summary of the Mystery of Redemption

86. And so the Heart of our Savior reflects in some way the image of the divine Person of the Word and, at the same time, of His twofold nature, the human and the divine; in it we can consider not only the symbol but, in a sense, the summary of the whole mystery of our redemption. When we adore the Sacred Heart of Jesus Christ, we adore in it and through it both the uncreated love of the divine Word and also its human love and its other emotions and virtues, since both loves moved our Redeemer to sacrifice Himself for us and for His Spouse, the Universal Church, as the

---

[673] Rom. 8:35, 37-39.

Apostle declares: "Christ loved the Church, and delivered Himself up for it, that He might sanctify it, cleansing it by the laver of water in the word of life, that He might present it to Himself a glorious Church, not having spot or wrinkle, or any such thing, but that it should be holy and without blemish."[674]

c) As Perpetual Advocate With the Father

87. Just as Christ loved the Church, so He still loves it most intensely with that threefold love of which We spoke, which moved Him as our Advocate[675] "always living to make intercession for us"[676] to win grace and mercy for us from His Father. The prayers which are drawn from that unfailing love, and are directed to the Father, never cease. As "in the days of His flesh,"[677] so now victorious in heaven, He makes His petition to His heavenly Father with equal efficacy, to Him "Who so loved the world that He gave His only begotten Son, that whosoever believeth in Him may not perish, but may have life everlasting,"[678] He shows His living Heart, wounded as it were, and throbbing with a love yet more intense than when it was wounded in death by the Roman soldier's lance: "(Thy Heart) has been wounded so that through the visible wound we may behold the invisible wound of love."[679]

88. It is beyond doubt, then, that His heavenly Father "Who spared not even His own Son, but delivered Him up for us all,"[680] when appealed to with such loving urgency by so powerful an Advocate, will, through Him, send down on all men an abundance of divine graces.

89. It was Our wish, Venerable Brethren, by this general outline, to set before you and the faithful the inner nature of the devotion to the Sacred Heart of Jesus Christ and the endless riches which spring from it as they are made clear by the primary source

---

[674] Eph. 5:25-27.
[675] Cf. 1Jn. 2:1.
[676] Heb. 7:25.
[677] Heb. 5:7.
[678] Jn. 3:16.
[679] Bonaventure, Opusc. X: *Vitis mystica*, III, 5, in: *Opera Omnia* (Ad Claras Aquas: Quaracchi, 1898), 8:164; cf. *Summa Theologiae* III, q. 54, art. 4.
[680] Rom. 8:32.

of doctrine, divine revelation. We think that Our comments, which are guided by the light of the Gospel, have proved that this devotion, summarily expressed, is nothing else than devotion to the divine and human love of the Incarnate Word and to the love by which the heavenly Father and the Holy Spirit exercise their care over sinful men. For, as the Angelic Doctor teaches, the love of the most Holy Trinity is the origin of man's redemption; it overflowed into the human will of Jesus Christ and into His adorable Heart with full efficacy and led Him, under the impulse of that love, to pour forth His blood to redeem us from the captivity of sin:[681] "I have a baptism wherewith I am to be baptized, and how am I straitened until it be accomplished?"[682]

4. Origin and Development of Devotion to the Heart of Jesus

a) In Early Christianity

90. We are convinced, then, that the devotion which We are fostering to the love of God and Jesus Christ for the human race by means of the revered symbol of the pierced Heart of the crucified Redeemer has never been altogether unknown to the piety of the faithful, although it has become more clearly known and has spread in a remarkable manner throughout the Church in quite recent times. Particularly was this so after our Lord Himself had privately revealed this divine secret to some of His children to whom He had granted an abundance of heavenly gifts, and whom He had chosen as His special messengers and heralds of this devotion.

91. But, in fact, there have always been men specially dedicated to God who, following the example of the beloved Mother of God, of the Apostles and the great Fathers of the Church, have practiced the devotion of thanksgiving, adoration and love towards the most sacred human nature of Christ, and especially towards the wounds by which His body was torn when He was enduring suffering for our salvation.

92. Moreover, is there not contained in those words "My Lord

---

[681] Cf. *Summa Theologiae* III, q. 48, art. 5.
[682] Lk. 12:50.

and My God"[683] which St. Thomas the Apostle uttered, and which showed he had been changed from an unbeliever into a faithful follower, a profession of faith, adoration and love, mounting up from the wounded human nature of his Lord to the majesty of the divine Person?

93. But if men have always been deeply moved by the pierced Heart of the Savior to a worship of that infinite love with which He embraces mankind—since the words of the prophet Zacharias, "They shall look on Him Whom they have pierced,"[684] referred by St. John the Evangelist to Jesus nailed to the Cross, have been spoken to Christians in all ages—it must yet be admitted that it was only by a very gradual advance that the honors of a special devotion were offered to that Heart as depicting the love, human and divine, which exists in the Incarnate Word.

b) Precursors in the Middle Ages

94. But for those who wish to touch on the more significant stages of this devotion through the centuries, if we consider outward practice, there immediately occur the names of certain individuals who have won particular renown in this matter as being the advance guard of a form of piety which, privately and very gradually, has gained more and more strength in religious congregations. To cite some examples in establishing this devotion to the Sacred Heart of Jesus and continuously promoting it, great service was rendered by St. Bonaventure, St. Albert the Great, St. Gertrude, St. Catherine of Siena, Blessed Henry Suso, St. Peter Canisius, St. Francis de Sales. St. John Eudes was responsible for the first liturgical office celebrated in honor of the Sacred Heart of Jesus whose solemn feast, with the approval of many Bishops in France, was observed for the first time on October 20, 1672.

c) The Revelations to Saint Margaret Mary

95. But surely the most distinguished place among those who have fostered this most excellent type of devotion is held by St. Margaret Mary Alacoque who, under the spiritual direction

[683] Jn. 20:28.
[684] Jn. 19:37; cf. Zach. 12:10.

of Blessed Claude de la Colombière who assisted her work, was on fire with an unusual zeal to see to it that the real meaning of the devotion which had had such extensive developments to the great edification of the faithful should be established and be distinguished from other forms of Christian piety by the special qualities of love and reparation.[685]

96. It is enough to recall the record of that age in which the devotion to the Sacred Heart of Jesus began to develop to understand clearly that its marvelous progress has stemmed from the fact that it entirely agreed with the nature of Christian piety since it was a devotion of love. It must not be said that this devotion has taken its origin from some private revelation of God and has suddenly appeared in the Church; rather, it has blossomed forth of its own accord as a result of that lively faith and burning devotion of men who were endowed with heavenly gifts, and who were drawn towards the adorable Redeemer and His glorious wounds which they saw as irresistible proofs of that unbounded love.

97. Consequently, it is clear that the revelations made to St. Margaret Mary brought nothing new into Catholic doctrine. Their importance lay in this: that Christ Our Lord, exposing His Sacred Heart, wished in a quite extraordinary way to invite the minds of men to a contemplation of, and a devotion to, the mystery of God's merciful love for the human race. In this special manifestation Christ pointed to His Heart, with definite and repeated words, as the symbol by which men should be attracted to a knowledge and recognition of His love; and at the same time He established it as a sign or pledge of mercy and grace for the needs of the Church of our times....

5. Church Teaching About the Nature of This Devotion

100. From what We have so far explained, Venerable Brethren, it is clear that the faithful must seek from Scripture, tradition and the sacred liturgy as from a deep untainted source, the devotion to the Sacred Heart of Jesus if they desire to penetrate its inner nature and by piously meditating on it, receive the nourishment for the

---

[685] Cf. the Encyclical *Miserentissimus Redemptor*, in AAS 20:167-168 (see Appendix 5).

fostering and development of their religious fervor. If this devotion is constantly practiced with this knowledge and understanding, the souls of the faithful cannot but attain to the sweet knowledge of the love of Christ which is the perfection of Christian life as the Apostle, who knew this from personal experience, teaches: "For this cause I bow my knees to the Father of our Lord Jesus Christ... that He may grant you, according to the riches of His glory, to be strengthened by His Spirit with might unto the inward man; that Christ may dwell by faith in your hearts; that, being rooted and founded in charity... you may be able to know also the charity of Christ which surpasseth all knowledge, that you may be filled unto all the fullness of God." [686] The clearest image of this all-embracing fullness of God is the Heart of Christ Jesus itself. We mean the fullness of mercy which is proper to the New Testament, in which "the goodness and kindness of God our Savior appeared," [687] for "God sent not His Son into the world to judge the world, but that the world might be saved by Him." [688]

a) This Cult is not Tainted by Materialism or Superstition

101. The Church, the teacher of men, has therefore always been convinced from the time she first published official documents concerning the devotion to the Sacred Heart of Jesus that its essential elements, namely, acts of love and reparation by which God's infinite love for the human race is honored, are in no sense tinged with so-called "materialism" or tainted with the poison of superstition. Rather, this devotion is a form of piety that fully corresponds to the true spiritual worship which the Savior Himself foretold when speaking to the woman of Samaria: "The hour cometh, and now is, when the true adorers shall adore the Father in spirit and in truth. For the Father also seeketh such to adore Him. God is a spirit; and they that adore Him must adore Him in spirit and in truth." [689]

102. It is wrong, therefore, to assert that the contemplation of the physical Heart of Jesus prevents an approach to a close love of God and holds back the soul on the way to the attainment of the highest virtues....

---

[686] Eph. 3:14, 16-19.

[687] Tit. 3:4.

[688] Jn. 3:17.

[689] Jn. 4:23-24.

b) It Unifies the Threefold Love: Sentimental, Spiritual and Infused Divine Charity

104. Thus, from something corporeal such as the Heart of Jesus Christ with its natural meaning, it is both lawful and fitting for us, supported by Christian faith, to mount not only to its love as perceived by the senses but also higher, to a consideration and adoration of the infused heavenly love; and finally, by a movement of the soul at once sweet and sublime, to reflection on, and adoration of, the divine love of the Word Incarnate. We do so since, in accordance with the faith by which we believe that both natures—the human and the divine—are united in the Person of Christ, we can grasp in our minds those most intimate ties which unite the love of feeling of the physical Heart of Jesus with that twofold spiritual love, namely, the human and the divine love. For these loves must be spoken of not only as existing side by side in the adorable Person of the divine Redeemer but also as being linked together by a natural bond insofar as the human love, including that of the feelings, is subject to the divine and, in due proportion, provides us with an image of the latter. We do not pretend, however, that we must contemplate and adore in the Heart of Jesus what is called the formal image, that is to say, the perfect and absolute symbol of His divine love, for no created image is capable of adequately expressing the essence of this love. But a Christian in paying honor along with the Church to the Heart of Jesus is adoring the symbol and, as it were, the visible sign of the divine charity which went so far as to love intensely, through the Heart of the Word made Flesh, the human race stained with so many sins.

c) The Twofold Goal: God's Love for us and our Love for God

105. It is therefore essential, at this point, in a doctrine of such importance and requiring such prudence that each one constantly hold that the truth of the natural symbol by which the physical Heart of Jesus is related to the Person of the Word, entirely depends upon the fundamental truth of the hypostatic union. Should anyone declare this to be untrue he would be reviving false opinions, more than once condemned by the Church, for they are opposed to the oneness of the Person of Christ even though the two natures are each complete and distinct.

106. Once this essential truth has been established we understand that the Heart of Jesus is the heart of a divine Person, the Word Incarnate, and by it is represented and, as it were, placed before our gaze all the love with which He has embraced and even now embraces us. Consequently, the honor to be paid to the Sacred Heart is such as to raise it to the rank—so far as external practice is concerned—of the highest expression of Christian piety. For this is the religion of Jesus which is centered on the Mediator who is man and God, and in such a way that we cannot reach the Heart of God save through the Heart of Christ, as He Himself says: "I am the Way, the Truth and the Life. No one cometh to the Father save [except] by Me."[690]

107. And so we can easily understand that the devotion to the Sacred Heart of Jesus, of its very nature, is a worship of the love with which God, through Jesus, loved us, and at the same time, an exercise of our own love by which we are related to God and to other men. Or to express it in another way, devotion of this kind is directed towards the love of God for us in order to adore it, give thanks for it, and live so as to imitate it; it has this in view, as the end to be attained, that we bring that love by which we are bound to God to the rest of men to perfect fulfillment by carrying out daily more eagerly the new commandment which the divine Master gave to His Apostles as a sacred legacy when He said: "A new commandment I give to you, that you love one another as I have loved you.... This is My commandment that you love one another as I have loved you."[691] And this commandment is really new and Christ's own, for as Aquinas says, "It is, in brief, the difference between the New and the Old Testament, for as Jeremias says, 'I will make a new covenant with the house of Israel.'[692] But that commandment which in the Old Testament was based on fear and reverential love was referring to the New Testament; hence, this commandment was in the old Law not really belonging to it, but as a preparation for the new Law."[693]

---

[690] Jn. 14:6.

[691] Jn. 13:34; 15:12.

[692] Jer. 31:31.

[693] *Commentaria in Evangelium* S. Ioannis, XIII, lect. VII, 3.

Conclusions

1. Appeal to practice this devotion

a) It is a Practice of the Virtue of Divine Worship
    108. Before We conclude Our treatment of the concept of this type of devotion and its excellence in Christian life, which We have offered for your consideration—a subject at once attractive and full of consolation—by virtue of the Apostolic office which was first entrusted to Blessed Peter after he had made his threefold profession of love, We think it opportune to exhort you once again venerable brethren, and through you all those dear children of Ours in Christ, to continue to exercise an ever more vigorous zeal in promoting this most attractive form of piety; for from it in our times also We trust that very many benefits will arise.
    109. In truth, if the arguments brought forward which form the foundation for the devotion to the pierced Heart of Jesus are duly pondered, it is surely clear that there is no question here of some ordinary form of piety which anyone at his own whim may treat as of little consequence or set aside as inferior to others, but of a religious practice which helps very much towards the attaining of Christian perfection.

b) One Fulfills Thereby the Demands of the Liturgy
    For if "devotion"—according to the accepted theological notion which the Angelic Doctor gives us—"appears to be nothing else save a willingness to give oneself readily to what concerns the service of God,"[694] is it possible that there is any service of God more obligatory and necessary, and at the same time more excellent and attractive, than the one which is dedicated to love? For what is more pleasing and acceptable to God than service which pays homage to the divine love and is offered for the sake of that love—since any service freely offered is a gift in some sense and love "has the position of the first gift, through which all other free gifts are made?"[695]

---

[694] *Summa Theologiae*, II-II, q. 82, art. 1.
[695] *Summa Theologiae*, I, q. 38, art. 1.

110. That form of piety, then, should be held in highest esteem by means of which man honors and loves God more and dedicates himself with greater ease and promptness to the divine charity; a form which our Redeemer Himself deigned to propose and commend to Christians and which the Supreme Pontiffs in their turn defended and highly praised in memorable published documents. Consequently, to consider of little worth this signal benefit conferred on the Church by Jesus Christ would be to do something both rash and harmful and also deserving of God's displeasure.

c) One Practices Thereby Unselfish Love

111. This being so, there is no doubt that Christians in paying homage to the Sacred Heart of the Redeemer are fulfilling a serious part of their obligations in their service of God and, at the same time, they are surrendering themselves to their Creator and Redeemer with regard to both the affections of the heart and the external activities of their life; in this way, they are obeying that divine commandment: "Thou shalt love the Lord thy God with thy whole heart, and with thy whole soul, and with thy whole mind, and with thy whole Strength."[696]

112. Besides, they have the firm conviction that they are moved to honor God not primarily for their own advantage in what concerns soul and body in this life and in the next, but for the sake of God's goodness they strive to render Him their homage, to give Him back love for love, to adore Him and offer Him due thanks. Were it not so, the devotion to the Sacred Heart of Jesus Christ would be out of harmony with the whole spirit of the Christian religion, since man would not direct his homage, in the first instance, to the divine love. And, not unreasonably as sometimes happens, accusations of excessive self-love and self-interest are made against those who either misunderstand this excellent form of piety or practice it in the wrong way.

Hence, let all be completely convinced that in showing devotion to the most Sacred Heart of Jesus the external acts of piety have not the first or most important place; nor is its essence to be

---

[696] Mk. 12:30; Mt. 22:37.

found primarily in the benefits to be obtained. For if Christ has solemnly promised them in private revelations it was for the purpose of encouraging men to perform with greater fervor the chief duties of the Catholic religion, namely, love and expiation, and thus take all possible measures for their own spiritual advantage.

d) This Cult is Founded on Scripture, Tradition and the Liturgy

113. We therefore urge all Our children in Christ, both those who are already accustomed to drink the saving waters flowing from the Heart of the Redeemer and, more especially those who look on from a distance like hesitant spectators, to eagerly embrace this devotion. Let them carefully consider, as We have said, that it is a question of a devotion which has long been powerful in the Church and is solidly founded on the Gospel narrative. It received clear support from tradition and the sacred liturgy and has been frequently and generously praised by the Roman Pontiffs themselves. These were not satisfied with establishing a feast in honor of the most Sacred Heart of the Redeemer and extending it to the Universal Church; they were also responsible for the solemn acts of dedication which consecrated the whole human race to the same Sacred Heart.[697]

e) It Produces Abundant Fruits of Conversion

114. Moreover, there are to be reckoned the abundant and joyous fruits which have flowed therefrom to the Church: countless souls returned to the Christian religion, the faith of many roused to greater activity, a closer tie between the faithful and our most loving Redeemer. All these benefits particularly in the most recent decades, have passed before Our eyes in greater numbers and more dazzling significance.

115. While We gaze round at such a marvelous sight, namely, a devotion to the Sacred Heart of Jesus both warm and widespread

---

[697] Cf. Leo XIII, *Encyclical Annum Sacrum, in: Acta Leonis,* 19 (1900): 71 ff.; Decree of the Sacred Congregation of Rites (28 June 1899), in: Decr. Auth., III, n. 3712; Encyclical *Miserentissimus Redemptor,* in: AAS (1928): 177 ff. (see Appendix 5); Decr. S.C. Rit. (29 January 1929), in: *AAS* 21 (1929): 77.

among all ranks of the faithful, We are filled with a sense of gratitude and joy and consolation. And after We have offered thanks, as We ought, to our Redeemer Who is the infinite treasury of goodness, We cannot help offering Our paternal congratulations to all those, whether of the clergy or of the laity, who have made active contribution to the extending of this devotion.

2. Special Usefulness of This Devotion for our Time

116. But although, venerable brethren, devotion to the Sacred Heart of Jesus has everywhere brought forth fruits of salvation for the Christian life, all are aware that the Church militant on earth—and especially civil society—has not yet attained in a real sense to its essential perfection which would correspond to the prayers and desires of Jesus Christ, the Mystical Spouse of the Church and Redeemer of the human race. Not a few children of the Church mar, by their too many sins and imperfections, the beauty of this Mother's features which they reflect in themselves. Not all Christians are distinguished by that holiness of behavior to which God calls them; not all sinners have returned to the Father's house, which they unfortunately abandoned, that they may be clothed once again with the "first robe"[698] and worthily receive on their finger the ring, the pledge of loyalty to the spouse of their soul; not all the heathen peoples have yet been gathered into the membership of the Mystical Body of Christ.

a) The Present Need of the Church

117. And there is more. For if We experience bitter sorrow at the feeble loyalty of the good in whose souls, tricked by a deceptive desire for earthly possessions, the fire of divine charity grows cool and gradually dies out, much more is Our heart deeply grieved by the machinations of evil men who, as if instigated by Satan himself, are now more than ever zealous in their open and implacable hatred against God, against the Church and above all against him who on earth represents the Person of the divine Redeemer and exhibits His love towards men, in accordance with that well-known saying of the Doctor of Milan: "For (Peter) is being questioned about that which

---

[698] Lk. 15:22.

is uncertain, though the Lord is not uncertain; He is questioning not that He may learn, but that He may teach the one whom, at His ascent into Heaven, He was leaving to us as 'the representative of His love.'"[699]

118. But, in truth, hatred of God and of those who lawfully act in His place is the greatest kind of sin that can be committed by man created in the image and likeness of God and destined to enjoy His perfect and enduring friendship for ever in heaven. Man, by hatred of God more than by anything else, is cut off from the Highest Good and is driven to cast aside from himself and from those near to him whatever has its origin in God, whatever is united with God, whatever leads to the enjoyment of God, that is, truth, virtue, peace and justice.[700]

119. Since then, alas, one can see that the number of those whose boast is that they are God's enemies is in some places increasing, that the false slogans of materialism are being spread by act and argument, and unbridled license for unlawful desires is everywhere being praised, is it remarkable that love, which is the supreme law of the Christian religion, the surest foundation of true and perfect justice and the chief source of peace and innocent pleasures, loses its warmth in the souls of many? For as our Savior warned us: "Because iniquity hath abounded, the charity of many shall grow cold."[701]

b) Devotion to the Sacred Heart Responds to This Need

120. When so many evils meet Our gaze—such as cause sharp conflict among individuals, families, nations and the whole world, particularly today more than at any other time—where are We to seek a remedy, venerable brethren? Can a form of devotion surpassing that to the most Sacred Heart of Jesus be found, which corresponds better to the essential character of the Catholic faith, which is more capable of assisting the present-day needs of the Church and the human race? What religious practice is more excellent, more

---

[699] Ambrose, *Expositio in Evangelium secundum Lucam,* I, 10, n. 175, in: PL 15, 1942.

[700] Cf. *Summa Theologiae,* II-II, q. 34, art. 2.

[701] Mt. 24:12.

attractive, more salutary than this, since the devotion in question is entirely directed towards the love of God itself?[702]

Finally, what more effectively than the love of Christ—which devotion to the Sacred Heart of Jesus daily increases and fosters more and more—can move the faithful to bring into the activities of life the Law of the Gospel, the setting aside of which, as the words of the Holy Spirit plainly warn, "the work of justice shall be peace,"[703] makes peace worthy of the name completely impossible among men?

121. And so, following in the footsteps of Our immediate predecessor, We are pleased to address once again to all Our dear sons in Christ those words of exhortation which Leo XIII, of immortal memory, towards the close of last century addressed to all the faithful and to all who were genuinely anxious about their own salvation and that of civil society: "Behold, today, another true sign of God's favor is presented to our gaze, namely, the Sacred Heart of Jesus . . . shining forth with a wondrous splendor from amidst flames. In it must all our hopes be placed; from it salvation is to be sought and hoped for."[704]

122. It is likewise Our most fervent desire that all who profess themselves Christians and are seriously engaged in the effort to establish the kingdom of Christ on earth will consider the practice of devotion to the Heart of Jesus as the source and symbol of unity, salvation and peace. Let no one think, however, that by such a practice anything is taken from the other forms of piety with which Christian people, under the guidance of the Church, have honored the divine Redeemer. Quite the opposite. Fervent devotional practice towards the Heart of Jesus will beyond all doubt foster and advance devotion to the Holy Cross in particular, and love for the Most Holy Sacrament of the Altar. We can even assert—as the revelations made by Jesus Christ to St. Gertrude and to St. Margaret Mary clearly show—that no one really ever has a proper understanding of Christ crucified to whom the inner mysteries of His Heart

---

[702] Cf. Encyclical *Miserentissimus Redemptor,* in: AAS 20 (1928): 166 (see Appendix 5).

[703] Isa. 32:17.

[704] Encyclical *Annum Sacrum,* in: *Acta Leonis* 19 (1900): 79; Encyclical *Miserentissimus Redemptor,* in AAS 20 (1928): 167 (see Appendix 5).

have not been made known. Nor will it be easy to understand the strength of the love which moved Christ to give Himself to us as our spiritual food save by fostering in a special way the devotion to the Eucharistic Heart of Jesus, the purpose of which is—to use the words of Our predecessor of happy memory, Leo XIII—"to call to mind the act of supreme love whereby our Redeemer, pouring forth all the treasures of His Heart in order to remain with us till the end of time, instituted the adorable Sacrament of the Eucharist."[705] For "not the least part of the revelation of that Heart is the Eucharist, which He gave to us out of the great charity of His own Heart."[706]

123. Finally, moved by an earnest desire to set strong bulwarks against the wicked designs of those who hate God and the Church and, at the same time, to lead men back again, in their private and public life, to a love of God and their neighbor, We do not hesitate to declare that devotion to the Sacred Heart of Jesus is the most effective school of the love of God; the love of God, We say, which must be the foundation on which to build the kingdom of God in the hearts of individuals, families, and nations, as that same predecessor of pious memory wisely reminds us: "The reign of Jesus Christ takes its strength and form from divine love: to love with holiness and order is its foundation and its perfection. From it these must flow: to perform duties without blame; to take away nothing of another's right; to guide the lower human affairs by heavenly principles; to give the love of God precedence over all other creatures."[707]

3. Honoring the Immaculate Heart of Mary

124. In order that favors in greater abundance may flow on all Christians, nay, on the whole human race, from the devotion to the most Sacred Heart of Jesus, let the faithful see to it that to this devotion the Immaculate Heart of the Mother of God is closely joined. For, by God's Will, in carrying out the work of human Redemption the Blessed Virgin Mary was inseparably

---

[705] *Litterae Apostolicae quibus Archisodalitas a Corde Eucharistico Jesu ad S. Ioachim de Urbe erigitur* (17 February 1903), in: Acta Leonis 22 (1903): 116.

[706] Albertus Magnus, *De Eucharistia,* dist. VI, tr. 1, c. 1, in: *Opera Omnia,* ed. Borgnet, vol. 38 (Paris, 1890), 358.

[707] Encyclical *Tametsi, in: Acta Leonis* 20 (1900): 303.

linked with Christ in such a manner that our salvation sprang from the love and the sufferings of Jesus Christ to which the love and sorrows of His Mother were intimately united. It is, then, entirely fitting that the Christian people—who received the divine life from Christ through Mary—after they have paid their debt of honor to the Sacred Heart of Jesus should also offer to the most loving Heart of their heavenly Mother the corresponding acts of piety affection, gratitude and expiation. Entirely in keeping with this most sweet and wise disposition of divine Providence is the memorable act of consecration by which We Ourselves solemnly dedicated Holy Church and the whole world to the spotless Heart of the Blessed Virgin Mary.[708]

4. The Centenary of the Institution of the Feast of the Sacred Heart

125. Since in the course of this year there is completed, as We mentioned above, the first hundred years since the Universal Church, by order of Our predecessor of happy memory, Pius IX, celebrated the feast of the Sacred Heart of Jesus, We earnestly desire, Venerable Brethren, that the memory of this centenary be everywhere observed by the faithful in the making of public acts of adoration, thanksgiving and expiation to the divine Heart of Jesus. And though all Christian peoples will be linked by the bonds of charity and prayer in common, ceremonies of Christian joy and piety will assuredly be carried out with a special religious fervor in that nation in which, according to the dispensation of the divine Will, a holy virgin pointed the way and was the untiring herald of that devotion.

126. Meanwhile, refreshed by sweet hope and foreseeing already those spiritual fruits which We are confident will spring up in abundance in the Church from the devotion to the Sacred Heart of Jesus—provided it is correctly understood according to Our explanation and actively put into practice—We make Our prayer to God that He may graciously deign to assist these ardent desires of Ours by the strong help of His grace. May it come about, by the divine inspiration as a token of His favor, that out of the celebration established for this year the love of the faithful may grow daily more and more towards the Sacred Heart of Jesus and its sweet and

---

[708] Cf. *AAS* 34 (1942): 345 ff.

sovereign kingdom be extended more widely to all in every part of the world: the kingdom "of truth and life; the kingdom of grace and holiness; the kingdom of justice, love and peace."[709]

127. As a pledge of these favors with a full heart We impart to each one of you, Venerable Brethren, together with the clergy and faithful committed to your charge, to those in particular who by their devoted labors foster and promote the devotion to the Sacred Heart of Jesus, Our apostolic benediction.

Given at Rome, at St. Peter's, the 15th of May, 1956, the eighteenth year of Our Pontificate.

PIUS XII, POPE

---

[709] From the Roman Missal, Preface for Christ the King.

Also Available from Loreto Publications
www.loretopubs.org
603-239-6671

The Sacred Heart Families Novena book
A special project of Loreto Publications
96 pages, soft-bound cover, $9.95
Over 100 years ago in Germany and in France thousands of families joined together in a prayer warrior project for several purposes, many related to political and social protections for their nations and their Catholic families. Fourteen families formed a group, which was organized by a committee formed for the purpose of facilitating communications. These families would each agree to pray this novena three times each year at a scheduled time, forming hundreds of rotating perpetual novenas to the incalculable benefit of their families, parishes and nations. Of course anyone, anywhere, anytime, may utilize this beautiful novena whether or not they are part of the Sacred Heart Families Novena league. This is the official Novena booklet recently translated from the German and French editions. It includes the novena itself, some explanations and exhortations and charts for keeping track of the families and their appointed times, as well as the address for joining or registering families or parish groups.

The Sacred Heart of Jesus
St. John Eudes, $16.95
Like Saint John the Apostle, Saint John Eudes had the privilege of what could be nothing less than direct intimate access to the Sacred Heart of Jesus and the Immaculate Heart of Mary. One can only conclude after reading this book on the Sacred Heart that here was more a seraph than a man, driven by the Holy Spirit to cast the fire of the Savior's love upon this earth with the pen of a scrivener lost in divine abandon. Surely, our Lord gave the key to the treasure house of His Heart to John Eudes. This book opens that treasure to the one with holy desires. God is wonderful in his saints, and with holy gusto we second the accolade given to him by a grateful generation: the wonder of his age.

Commentary on Holy Scripture
by Cornelius aLapide